Magic Guidebooks:
Disneyland®
2017

Secrets, Money Saving Tips, Hidden Mickeys, and Everything Else You Need to Know in a Single Guide!

Text © 2017 Magic Guides: Theme Park Travel. All Rights Reserved.

This book and its publisher are not affiliated with the Walt Disney Company or the Walt Disney World Resort®. All rides and attraction names are property of or copyright of the Walt Disney Company and we do not claim copyright over any of the rides, movies, or attractions mentioned in this guide. None of the images in this guide represent the Walt Disney World Resort® and they are original or have been properly licensed.

This book is presented solely for educational and entertainment purposes. The author and publisher are not offering it as legal, accounting, or other professional services advice. While best efforts have been used in preparing this book, the author and publisher make no representations or warranties of any kind and assume no liabilities of any kind with respect to the accuracy or completeness of the contents. Neither the author nor the publisher shall be held liable or responsible to any person or entity with respect to any loss or incidental or consequential damages caused, or alleged to have been caused, directly or indirectly, by the information or guides contained herein.

Although the author and publisher have made every effort to ensure that the information in this book was correct at press time, the author and publisher do not assume and hereby disclaim any liability to any party for any loss, damage, or disruption caused by errors or omissions, whether such errors or omissions result from negligence, accident, or any other cause. Every company is different and the advice and strategies contained herein may not be suitable for your situation. Our recommendations are not necessarily an assertion that you must do so or that one company is better than another. We will give tips based on our experiences, but always encourage you to do some research before purchasing through a third party company or hotel.

Some of the content of this book is subject to change as attractions may close, prices may raise, menus change, character greeting spots move, etc. The publisher cannot hold responsibility if some of the content in this book is inaccurate.

Want even more tips and stunning photos of Disney Parks? Sign up for our Free E-Mail List on our Website:

www.magicguidebooks.com

You can also follow us on social media:

Instagram
@magicguides

Facebook
facebook.com/MagicGuides

Twitter
@magicguidebooks

We'd LOVE if you hashtag us!
#MagicGuidebooks

4

Magic Guidebooks:

Disneyland 2017

The Absolute, Best Disneyland Advice from the Experts!

Insider tips on using FastPass
and other tricks to skip the lines!

Save on Disneyland Resort hotels,
flights, and park tickets.

Reviews on restaurants, the best food,
and advice for saving money

Covers Disneyland, Disney California Adventure,
Downtown Disney, and beyond.

Table of Contents

About This Guide 8

Chapter 1: Introduction to the Disneyland Resort 9

Chatper 2: Disneyland Phrases and Resources 12

Chapter 3: Why Visit Disneyland in 2017 12

Chapter 4: Planning Your Disneyland Resort Vacation 20

Chapter 5: Booking Your Disneyland Vacation 36

Chapter 6: Traveling to the Resort 42

Chapter 7: What to Wear and Bring (and What Not to) 48

Chapter 8: Hotel Guide 53

Chapter 9: Disneyland 70

Chapter 10: Disney California Adventure 101

Chapter 11: Downtown Disney 123

Chapter 12: Disney Character Locations 129

Chapter 13: Family with Kids 133

Chapter 14: Adult Guide to the Disneyland Resort 148

Chapter 15: A Non-Rider's Guide 159

Chapter 16: FastPass® and Single Rider Line Locations 163

Chapter 17: Tips for Getting Free Stuff 167

Chapter 18: The Best of the Disneyland: Top 8 Lists 169

Chapter 19: Hidden Mickeys 174

Chapter 20: Disneyland Legends 180

Pre-Planned Ride and Attractions Lists 186

Custom Ride List 199

Checklist 201

Index 202

Conclusion 209

About This Guide

When writing and designing this book, we had *you* in mind. Maybe you're a first-time visitor to the Disneyland Resort® or perhaps, you've frequented for many years. Wherever you come from and whatever your experience, we wanted to provide a complete guide from start to finish, while giving a critique of the attractions and restaurants in the resort. In fact, the entire purpose of this guide is to inform, critique, and recommend to you about the many attractions, restaurants, hotels, and more from the Disneyland Resort®.

Keep in mind that this guide is an "unofficial edition", meaning that we are in no way affiliated with the Walt Disney Company®, the Disneyland Resort®, the Walt Disney World® Resort, and nor have we ever been. We are simply fans of the Disneyland Resort® who are giving an honest opinion on what it has to offer.

-Magic Guides

Chapter One
Introduction to the Disneyland Resort

"The Happiest Place on Earth"

The Disneyland Resort in California is home to virtually countless attractions, thrilling and classic rides, and gourmet food perfect for people of all ages. With two breath-taking theme parks (Disneyland and Disney California Adventure), three open-property hotels, and a dazzling Downtown Disney for shopping and restaurants, it's no wonder that millions of people flock there from all over the world! So why is it "The Happiest Place on Earth"? The truth is, no matter our age, Disneyland brings us back to feeling like a kid again in a place that allows us to be! From world-class rides, stunning fireworks, delicious food, lands for kids, and bars for adults, the Disneyland Resort has it all! In short, whether you like thrilling state-of-the-art rides like *Indiana Jones* and *Space Mountain* or seeing a spectacular show like *World of Color* or *Paint the Night*, you will be floored by Disneyland's magic.

So, Why Do I Need a Book?

While you can go to the Disneyland Resort and attempt to take all of the experiences on your own, having tips from insiders is priceless. This guide will save you time waiting in lines, money, and give you the best options to fit your mood. We visit the Disneyland Resort more times in a year than we can count and we know all the ins and outs of the parks.

Whether you are looking to ride all of the thrill rides in one day, two days, or don't like rides at all, this book will be your guide. Whether you are visiting with kids, other adults, or even by yourself, we've got you covered! Packed with insider secrets (we call them "Magic Tips") on where to get the best food, little-known experiences, hidden adventures, and more, this book will be your ultimate guide to the Disneyland Resort!

I've Been to Disney World... Should I Still Visit Disneyland?

As native Southern Californians, Disneyland has a special place in our hearts. Truthfully, we believe that there is a magic in the Disneyland Resort that doesn't exist at any other park. While we *love* Disney World, Walt Disney created Disneyland himself (he sadly passed before Walt Disney World was completed), and the magic residing in the Disneyland Park comes from Walt himself.

The cast members (Disney employees) are always helpful and friendly and the parks are impeccably clean! Sure, many of the rides are similar in both Resorts, like *Pirates of the Caribbean* and *Big Thunder Mountain Railroad*, but the Disneyland Resort exists with more detail in the parks that create a magic unlike anywhere else.

We will add that the Disney World castle is much larger (over 100 feet taller than the Sleeping Beauty Castle in California), and many Disney World fanatics notice this first. However, Disneyland and Disney California Adventure have unique rides not found anywhere else like the Matterhorn Bobsleds, Cars Land, Indiana Jones Adventure, the seasonal Haunted Mansion Holiday starring the characters from Tim Burton's *The Nightmare Before Christmas*, to name a few. Even better, Disneyland and Disney California Adventure are located right across from one another, so no hauling on busses from park to park like at Walt Disney World.

How Many Days Should I Spend at the Disneyland Resort?

Between Disneyland, Disney California Adventure, and Downtown Disney, there appear to be countless attractions to visit. We'd recommend anywhere from two to four days to satisfy a trip.

If you want to stay longer, there is plenty to do! In this guide, we will show you how to experience Disneyland and California Adventure in one day, two days, three days, a week or more based on our suggestions, pre-planned ride list, and reviews of the Resort's attractions, and delicious dining.

Chapter Two
Disneyland Phrases and Resources

Introduction

If you are new to the Disney theme parks or just haven't been in some time, you'll instantly notice the vibrant lingo that arises at the parks. Whether you're talking to a fellow guest, cast member, or reading signs by rides, it helps to know the terms first. Secondly, we have our own terms that we use frequently throughout this book. They are fairly intuitive, but so that we are all on the same page (excuse the book pun), we invite you to familiarize yourself with the section to help with reading this guide.

Phrases and Words for this Guide Book

★ **Magic Tips** ★ - These are special tips and secrets from our personal experience after visiting the Disneyland Resort several times a year.
 The Magic Tips are designed to:
  • Save time waiting in lines
  • Get the best viewing areas for shows and parades
  • Save money booking
  • And *a lot* more! We love Disneyland and want to share our resort and theme park secrets with you!

Top Choice! - Found on our Top 8 List of most-recommended restaurants and eateries.

Ride Levels

Thrill Riders – Those looking for the maximum thrill of the rides. The Disneyland Resort doesn't have "extreme rides" (only one ride, California Screamin', has a loop), but instead the parks offer "themed rides" that add magic to their attractions that Thrill Riders will enjoy.

Everyone – Perfect for anyone of all ages, even many Thrill Riders enjoy these attractions.

Family – Suited for anyone of all ages, both kids and adults. However, these rides may not interest Thrill Riders.

Kids – Designed for kids ages 6-10.

Young Kids – Designed for young kids 2-5.

Restaurant Types

Table service – Restaurants with a waiter. It is suggested you that you tip based on the service you receive.

Fast Service – Meals that you can order and typically seat right away.

Cafeteria Style – Serve yourself from a selection of items and pay before you eat. These spaces often have ample bench seating.

"On-The-Go" Meal – This may be self-explanatory, but some of the meals in Disney are packed and ready to go. These are often meals you eat while watching a show in preferred seating.

Restaurant Pricing:

$ - Under $10 (typically snack carts)
$$ - $10 - $15 (typically Fast Service Restaurants)
$$$ - $15 - $25 (more expensive Fast Service Restaurants)
$$$$ - $25 or more (premium dining like the Blue Bayou and Carthay Circle)

Phrases and Words for the Disneyland Resort

The Disneyland Resort - The area that encompasses both theme parks (Disneyland and Disney California Adventure), Downtown Disney, the 3 hotels, and the parking lots.

Cast Member - A term for all Disney employees. We find that the Disneyland Resort cast members are the friendliest of them all!

Park Hopper - A ticket that allows you to visit both Disneyland and Disney California Adventure as many times as you'd like during that day.

"Dark Ride" - An indoor ride where the vehicle is guided along a track. Typically, these are family-friendly rides like "it's a small world" and "They also have air conditioning to escape the heat on hot days!

FastPass® - An easy and free way to cut the lines! FastPass kiosks are set up throughout Disneyland and Disney California Adventure near most popular attractions. Simply insert your park ticket and a FastPass will be distributed to you for the corresponding ride.

Single Rider Line – A fast way to get on the rides as long as you don't mind traveling by yourself.
Note: We've included a complete list of rides with FastPass and Single Rider Lines in Chapter Sixteen on page 234.

Passholders – Those who purchased Annual Passes.

3D – The use of 3D glasses during the ride or attraction.

4D – The use of 3D glasses with added effects like splashing water and rumbling seats.

Closed for Refurbishment – No one likes seeing this sign as it means that the ride is closed for restoration. Some refurbishments can last a couple of days, while others have lasted two years. The Disneyland Resort plans their refurbishments carefully and will post these on the entertainment schedule:
https://disneyland.disney.go.com/calendars/day

Contact Information

Disneyland.com
Visit for booking and reservations.

Hotel Reservations
(714) 781-6425
https://disneyland.disney.go.com/hotels

Disney Dining
Book your restaurant reservations in advance.

(714) 781-DINE
https://disneyland.disney.go.com/dining

Tickets - book your tickets in advance
(714) 781-4565
https://disneyland.disney.go.com/tickets

Other Booking Websites with Discounts

DisneyRewards.com - If you have a Disney Visa® Card, earn points and claim special rewards.

Orbitz.com/deals - For special promotions (look for codes up to 15% Off hotels).

Bookit.com/coupon-codes - Search here for discounts on flights, hotels, and ticket bundles.

Amextravel.com - If you have an American Express Card, this can save you, plus earn more rewards.

Costcotravel.com - If you have a Costco Membership, you might save big on vacation packages and tickets.

CoportatePerks.com - If you have a discount with your company, this site often has discounted tickets and Park Hopper options.

Chapter Three
Why Visit Disneyland in 2017?

Introduction

Whether you've been to the Disneyland Resort before or not, there are several new attractions that will make 2017 a special year to visit. With new rides and returning classics, 2017 will be a big standout year for the Disneyland Resort!

New Attractions

Guardians of the Galaxy – Mission: Breakout
Disney California Adventure
The popular Twilight Zone Tower of Terror is being transformed into Disneyland's first Marvel-themed ride. Guests will plummet over a dozen stories as they attempt to escape The Collector's evil grasp! Mission: Breakout opens Spring 2017!

Beat the Crowds Before Star Wars Land
Disneyland
Star Wars is coming to the Disneyland Resort in the largest way imaginable. Several acres of the Disneyland theme park have gone under construction to make way for likely the most-anticipated themed land since the Wizarding World of Harry Potter at Universal Orlando.

Star Wars Land (which is just a code name because Disney hasn't announced the official title yet) isn't set to open until around 2019 or 2020. However, we don't recommend waiting until then. Disneyland has so much to offer that it'll blow your socks off! Visit now before the insane crowds take over during the Star Wars Land launch. Plus, there are plenty of Star Wars-themed attractions in Tomorrowland like Star Tours and Hyperspace Mountain. Oh, and if you're extra curious, you'll be able to see the amazing Star Wars construction coming along as you ride Big Thunder Mountain Railroad.

Returning Attractions

Main Street Electrical Parade
Disneyland
See all of the lights and dazzling fun of Disneyland's famous nighttime parade. A line up of classic characters twirl to an electric track as the parade returns to the Disneyland Resort, possibly for its final time. There is no end date on the Main Street Electrical Parade, however, it will likely be replaced by Paint the Night by Summer of 2017.

More Openings
Disneyland
Fantasmic!, Tom Sawyer's Island, the Canoes, and the Disneyland Railroad all make a comeback after extensive construction. Be prepared for classic scenes and new touches coming in Spring 2017.

New Rides

Star Wars: Season of the Force
Disneyland
Tomorrowland has transformed into "Season of the Force" with Star Wars music, characters, and new takes on classic attractions! Each of these attractions is only around for a limited time.

Hyperspace Mountain
Disneyland
Hop aboard a Space Mountain rocket ship and blast into a "galaxy far, far away" while Tie Fighters and Rebel Starships blast lasers among the stars. It's the classic Space Mountain rollercoaster in the dark with added *Star Wars* special effects and music! This limited-time attraction was new for 2016 and will hopefully continue throughout 2017. However, from September until Halloween, Hyperspace Mountain will likely change to Space Mountain Ghost Galaxy, a haunted take on the classic ride without the Star Wars features.

Chapter Four
Planning Your Disneyland Resort Vacation

When to Visit the Disneyland Resort

Wanting to go to Disneyland is easy – planning it can be a whole other animal! The good news is, we're here to help. We've been to the Disneyland Resort more than we can count and we've picked up hundreds of useful tips for you. In this part of the guide, we will walk you through the choices of travel and our recommendations for saving time and money.

Choosing a time for your vacation may not be entirely up to you. It could depend on your work schedule, your travel schedule, or your children's vacation days from school. Whether you have flexible travel days or not, we have laid out a month-by-month breakdown of what to expect when you visit the Disneyland Resort. We also give you tips on how to avoid the long lines and more to save you time and make your stay a very enjoyable one!

Most Recommended Travel Months

1. **September** – Summer continues throughout September in Southern California. Expect hot days and far less crowds than in June, July, and August. Halloween begins mid-September!

2. **October** - Disneyland and Disney California Adventure come alive during Halloween with typically perfect weather. Decorations, desserts, special rides, and Mickey's Halloween Party await you!

3. **February** - The Disneyland Resort typically has fewer crowds at this time, though weekends can be busy.

Least Recommended Travel Months

1. **July** - Massive crowds from all over the world flood Disneyland. Expect higher ticket prices, long lines, and very hot weather.

2. **December** - While park guests are treated to the holiday decorations, treats, and special rides, the crowds are some of the most massive. If you must go in December, we recommend the first week.

3. **August** - Similar to July with the crowds, but August thins out in the last week when the kids get back to school. Keep in mind that the weather is blazing hot in Southern California at that time.

Are you planning to be at the resort during one of our least recommended months? Don't worry! This guide will help you avoid those long lines. Be sure to follow one of our pre-planned attraction lists - we use them ourselves and they can save you hours of time waiting in lines (or avoid them altogether). Tips for beating the crowds are at the end of this chapter.

Day Breakdown

Note: These days always depend on the month, but this is a general idea of how to avoid the largest crowds.

Sunday – Weekend crowds, but far less than Saturday.

Monday – Often these can be just as crowded as Sundays because people take off extra days to avoid weekend traffic. On Monday holidays, expect larger crowds, sometimes busier than weekends.

Tuesday – Our most recommended day for fewest crowds.

Wednesday – Our second most recommended day for fewest crowds.

Thursday – Third most recommended day for fewest crowds.

Friday – Less busy in the morning, but busiest in the evening after school is out for the Annual Passholders.

Saturday – The busiest day at the resort.

Holidays – It's best to avoid the busy holidays and three day weekends. The weekend from Friday through Tuesday will often be extremely busy during these times.

Best Days to Visit

- The 1st or 2nd weeks in February (especially Tuesdays and Wednesdays)
- The last week in January (unless it's near the Martin Luther King, Jr. Day Holiday on the 3rd Monday of January)
- 2nd week of September (but not around Labor Day)

Most Crowded Days

1. Christmas Day (and week)
2. New Year's Eve/Day
3. Thanksgiving week
4. Memorial Day weekend
5. Fourth of July
6. Labor Day weekend
7. Veterans Day

★ **Magic Tip** ★

Disneyland's new tier pricing will be higher (Peak pricing) on more crowded days and lower (Value pricing) on less crowded days.

Visit the ticketing website disneyland.disney.go.com/tickets for Value, Regular, and Peak pricing.

Month Breakdown

January

- **Overview:** January is busy in the first two weeks, and generally less busy after that. The first week will be crowded from and filled with holiday rides, treats, music, and decorations lighting the resort.
- **Weather:** mid-60°F (15°C) during the day and chilly at night
- **Least Crowded Days:** last week in January
- **Most Crowded:** first two weeks (especially around New Years) and Martin Luther King Jr. Weekend (Friday through Tuesday)
- **Holiday Rides and Attractions:**
    1. Haunted Mansion Holiday (Tim Burton's *The Nightmare Before Christmas*)
    2. "it's a small world" Holiday
    3. Jingle Cruise (Jungle Cruise Holiday)
    4. World of Color – Winter Dreams
    5. Meet Santa Claus at Elias & Co.

★ **Magic Tips** ★

Holiday rides typically continue through January 6th. Disneyland and Disney California Adventure may have ride closures for refurbishments after the holiday decorations come down.

February

- **Overview:** Possibly the least crowded month to visit the Disneyland Resort. Like January, the weather is cooler, and some of the rides may be in refurbishment.
- **Weather:** Low-70°F (21°C) during the day and chilly at night. However, February has been known to have heatwaves, bring the weather above 90°F (32°C).
- **Least Crowded Days:** Any week except near President's Day Weekend (Friday through Tuesday)
- **Most Crowded:** President's Day Weekend (Friday through Tuesday)

★ **Magic Tip** ★ Disneyland and Disney California Adventure may have more ride closures for refurbishments in February than other months.

March

- **Overview:** March's popularity has increased recently as spring breaks spread throughout the month. If you visit in March, be sure to do so during the week, Tuesday through Thursday.
- **Weather:** mid-70°F (21°C) during the day and chilly at night. However, March has been known to have occasional heatwaves, bring the weather above 90°F (32°C).
- **Least Crowded Days:** the first Tuesday, Wednesday, and Thursday of March.
- **Most Crowded:** Last two weeks of the month.

Deals:
- Disneyland Resort hotels will often have discounted pricing during this time.

- Southern Californians can enjoy discounts on multi-day tickets.

★ **Magic Tip** ★
Like February, Disneyland and Disney California Adventure may have some ride closures for refurbishments.

April

- **Overview:** With spring breaks continuing through April, the end of the month tends to be the least crowded.
- **Weather:** Mid-70°F (21°C) during the day and chilly at night.
- **Least Crowded Days:** The last two weeks of the month.
- **Most Crowded:** First two weeks of the month.
- **Special Days:**
    Bats Day – (April 29 - May 1st) – Goths (typically dressed in black) from far and wide venture to the park for this weekend. For more information, visit www.BatsDay.net.
- **Note:** April is also subject to ride refurbishments.

Deals:
- Disneyland Resort hotels will often have discounted pricing during this time.
- Southern Californians can enjoy discounts on multi-day tickets.

May

- **Overview:** Spring in Disneyland is beautiful with the sun and toward the end of the month, it will already feel like Summer.
- **Weather:** Mid-70°F (21°C) during the day and sometimes chilly at night.
- **Least Crowded Days:** The first two weeks of the month.
- **Most crowded:** Memorial Day weekend (Friday through Tuesday).

Special Days:
Bats Day – (April 29 - May 1st) – See April for details.
Dapper Day – Spring (May 1st) – See guests dressed in their "Sunday Best" on this unofficial, yet widely celebrated day. If you are interested in participating, visit: DapperDay.com for more details. This semi-annual day also occurs in November.

★ **Magic Tip** ★
May is also subject to ride refurbishments, but they usually wrap up before Memorial Day.

Deals:
- Disneyland Resort hotels will often have discounted pricing during this time.
- Southern Californians can enjoy discounts on multi-day tickets.

June

- **Overview:** The warm June weather perfectly suits the Disneyland Resort.
- **Weather:** Mid-80°F (27°C) during the day. Typically keeps warm at night.
- **Least crowded days:** Tuesday, Wednesdays, and Thursdays and the first week of the month.
- **Most crowded:** The last week of the month.

Deals: Disneyland Resort hotels will often have discounted pricing during this time.

★ **Magic Tip** ★
June is a bit of an unpredictable crowd month as school are closed and summer vacations begin.

July

- **Overview:** The weather heats up (sometimes unbearably so) and crowds from all over the world venture into the Disneyland Resort during July.
- **Weather:** High-80°F (27°C) during the day. Typically keeps warm at night.
- **Least Crowded Days:** Tuesday, Wednesdays, and Thursdays (unless one is July 4th)
- **Most Crowded:** July 4th

Note: If you are planning to visit in July, see our tips for beating the crowds at the end of this chapter.

August

- **Overview:** The weather continues to heat up even more in August as crowds continue to pour in until school begins.
- **Weather:** Mid-90°F (32°C) during the day. Typically keeps very warm at night.
- **Least Crowded Days:** Tuesday, Wednesdays, and Thursdays and the last two weeks of the month.
- **Most Crowded:** The first 2 weeks of the month.

September

- **Overview:** More hot weather typically all month long with Halloween rides and treats beginning mid-September.
- **Weather:** High-90°F (32°C) during the day. Typically keeps very warm at night.
- **Least Crowded Days:** Tuesday, Wednesdays, Thursdays, and Fridays (except for Mickey's Halloween Party nights)
- **Most Crowded:** Labor Day weekend.

- **Special Days:**
  Gay Days (September 30 - October 2nd) – An unofficial event for LGBT families and singles to wear red in the parks. Visit www.gaydaysanaheim.com for more information.

Note: See October for Disneyland Halloween details.

October

- **Overview:** October is a favorite time of ours at the Disneyland Resort! The weather cools down as the Halloween party kicks into full gear.
- **Weather:** Low-80°F (27°C) during the day, cools at night.
- **Least Crowded Days:** Tuesday, Wednesdays, and Thursdays
- **Most Crowded:** Halloween and Mickey's Halloween Party nights on select dates.

Halloween at the Disneyland Resort:
Mickey's Halloween Party begins! A perfect time to dress in costume (all ages) and get some treats. This is a specialty ticket and is not included with a standard ticket. See Disneyland.com for dates.

Halloween Holiday Rides and Attractions:
- Haunted Mansion Holiday – Jack Skellington and his friends from Tim Burton's *The Nightmare Before Christmas* take over the Haunted Mansion. The attraction features new animatronics, special effects, and music through January 6th.
- Space Mountain: Ghost Galaxy – a terrifying ghost follows you throughout the ride!
- Frightfully Fun Parade – a ghastly parade inspired by Disney Villains and hosted by Jack Skellington!
- See massive Mickey-shaped pumpkins, try delicious treats, and see your favorite characters dressed in their Halloween costumes!

Halloween Treat Highlights:
- Pumpkin Flan – Rancho del Zocalo Restaurante (Frontierland)

- Bat Mickey Cookie – Market House (Main Street, U.S.A.)
- Pumpkin Twist – Maurice's Treats (Fantasyland)
- Pumpkin Muffin, Pumpkin Spice Latte, and Pumpkin Cheesecake – Jolly Holiday Bakery Café (Main Street, U.S.A.)
- Halloween Premium Cone – Gibson Girl Ice Cream Parlor (Main Street, U.S.A.)

Special Days:

Gay Days (September 30 - October 2nd) – See September for details.

★ Magic Tip ★

Mickey's Halloween Party can be packed! To avoid some of these crazy times, book your tickets during the first half of the event dates.

November

- **Overview:** The holidays begin mid-November at the Disneyland Resort. Expect larger crowds beginning Veterans Day and forward.
  See for December for Disneyland Holiday details.
- **Weather:** Mid-70°F (21°C) during the day, cools at night to 50°F (10°C).
- **Least Crowded Days:** The first week of the month.
- **Most Crowded:** Veteran's Day and Thanksgiving week.

- **Special Days:**
  Dapper Day – Autumn (November 6th) – see guests dressed in their "Sunday Best" on this unofficial, yet widely celebrated day (also occurs in May). If you are interested in participating, visit: DapperDay.com for more details.

December

- **Overview:** The holidays are in full gear at the Disneyland Resort. See decorations all around with special treats, fun holiday-themed rides, and a chance to meet Santa Claus!
- **Weather:** Low-60°F (15°C) during the day, can cool at night to mid-40°F (5°C).
- **Least Crowded Days:** The first week of the month.
- **Most Crowded:** The last two weeks, especially Christmas Day and New Year's Eve.

Holidays at the Disneyland Resort:
See the glittering lights decorating the Disneyland Resort. From magnificent Christmas trees to endless strings of lights and ornaments, you'll be in awe of the resort's holiday transformation!

Holiday Rides and Attractions:
- Haunted Mansion Holiday - Jack Skellington and his friends from Tim Burton's *The Nightmare Before Christmas* continue their takeover of the Haunted Mansion. The attraction features new animatronics, special effects, and music through January 6th.
- "Jingle Cruise" - The Jungle Cruise get a Christmas layover with holiday humor and decorations around the riverboat ride.
- "it's a small world" holiday - See the magnificent lights that illuminate this classic attraction on the outside. Inside, see the wondrous holidays celebrated all around the world set to holiday music.
- A Christmas Fantasy Parade (Disneyland) - Mickey, Santa, Disney Princesses celebrate Christmas aboard stunning floats.
- World of Color: Winter Dreams (Disney California Adventure) - light up the night with a spectacular water show perfectly designed for the holiday season. Watch your favorite Disney characters come to life and celebrate the joy of the season.
- Meet Santa Claus in Critter Country (Disneyland) or Elias & Co. (Disney California Adventure) and meet Mickey and his friends in their holiday clothing. Don't forget to say hi to Jack Skellington and Sally near the Haunted Mansion Holiday!

Holiday Treat Highlights:

- Praline Cheese Cake - French Market Restaurant (New Orleans Square)
- Holiday Crispy (rice crispy) - Bengal Barbecue (Frontierland) and Refreshment Corner (Main Street, U.S.A.)
- Holiday Peppermint Mocha - Café Orleans and Blue Bayou Restaurant (New Orleans Square)
- Peppermint Ice Cream (candy cane cones also available) - Gibson Girl Ice Cream Parlor (Main Street, U.S.A.)

- <u>Gingerbread Man Cookie</u> - Golden Horseshoe (Frontierland)
- <u>Yule Logs</u> (Pumpkin and Chocolate Coffee) - Plaza Inn Restaurant (Main Street, U.S.A.)
- <u>Eggnog Latte</u> - Royal Street Veranda (New Orleans Square)
- <u>Holiday Brownie and Snowman Shortbread Cookie</u> - Village Haus Restaurant (Fantasyland)

Tips for Beating the Crowds (Even on the Busiest Days)

1. **Be Early** - Get to the park at open before the crowds. You will thank us for this tip when you see how effective it is!
2. **Plan Your Day** - Follow one of our pre-set day plans (or make your own). We use these planners ourselves and it will save you hours of time waiting in lines (many times you'll miss the long lines altogether).

3. **Use FastPass** – As early as possible, get passes to the rides that you want to experience.
4. **Avoid Typical Meal Times:**
   a. Lunch: Dine before 11.30am and after 2.30pm
   b. Dinner: Dine before 5.00pm and after 7.30pm
5. **Book Dining Reservations** – Reservations can be made at Disneyland.com 60 days in advance.
6. **Move to Disney California Adventure** – Disneyland can have many larger crowds than Disney California Adventure, especially in the morning. If the crowds are too much at Disneyland, head to the opposite park and see what you can ride or see there.
7. **You Might Have to Wait** – Waiting in line isn't the end of the world. Sometimes we all have to do it for the best attractions. The trick is to wait the *shortest* amount of time for the *fewest* rides possible. You can avoid the longest lines by following our planned out ride lists in Chapter Twenty.
8. **Take a Break** – If you are feeling worn out, take a break at your hotel or visit Downtown Disney. The resort offers so many surprises that you might have blast drinking a cup of coffee while you listen to music near Starbucks rather than surrounded by a swarm of people. After you and your group have recharged, head back into the parks.

Chapter Five
Booking Your Disneyland Vacation

Tips for Before You Book:

Pre-book your Hotel:
The further out you book your hotel, the less expensive it tends to be. Please refer to our Hotels Overview (Chapter 8) to read our hotel recommendations.

Fly into LAX (Los Angeles International):
If you are planning to fly, we recommend LAX because it tends to be the least expensive and easiest to travel from. LAX is located right next to highways that will take you to Disneyland.

Bundle:
Sometimes purchasing a flight/hotel/car package from Disneyland.com or third party travel website can save you a lot of money.

Know the Ticket Pricing Structure:
- Park tickets vary in pricing for each day.
- Tickets are broken into 3 categories:
	Value: $95 (typically Monday - Thursday)
	Regular: $105 (typically Friday - Sunday)
	Peak: $119 (holiday weeks, summer, spring break)
- Park Hoppers are an extra $50 - $60 for a single day.

- You can save on both parks by booking consecutive days.
- Visit: https://disneyland.disney.go.com/tickets for specific pricing for the dates you've chosen.

In this chapter, we outline how to save money on tickets, but for standard pricing, book at www.Disneyland.com.

Booking Discounts

There are many ways to save on booking your stay at the Disneyland Resort. Some are better than others depending on the offer. Here are our most recommended choices based on how much they can save you:

Bookit.com (877-742-9891) – *highly recommended!*

- Perfect for flying/hotel packages with ticket options.

- Benefits of booking at Bookit.com:
    - Payment plans available with a down payment (no credit check required).
    - Often big discounts on flights when you book a package.
    - Disneyland Resort Hotels Available (get all of the benefits including Extra Magic Hours and private park entry even when you book through a 3rd party site).
    - We tend to notice that Bookit.com has a different selection of available hotel rooms than other 3rd party sites.
    - Lists Disneyland's "Good Neighbor Hotels" so you can see the closest hotels for what Disneyland recommends.
    - Bundle park tickets for slight discounts. Save on multiday park hopper tickets and to other parks including Universal Studios Hollywood.

- ○ Discounted car rental options and inexpensive travel insurance available.

- Cons:
    - ○ When you just book a hotel without airfare, this website can sometimes be more expensive than other 3rd parties.
    - ○ Some of the better deals cannot be cancelled.
    - ○ Often the cancellation comes with a fee. Many other companies offer free cancellation without a fee. Bookit.com sometimes offers free cancellation, too.
    - ○ Promo Code: www.bookit.com/coupon-codes

Disneyland.com (714-520-5060)

- Check the website for discounts on hotels and more. Here you can book any of the 3 resort hotels, purchase tickets, and add features.
- Spring Time (March – June) typically has the lowest fares.
- When Disneyland.com has sales, usually the 3rd party websites will as well.

- Benefits of booking at Disneyland.com
    - ○ Just put $200.00 down when you book for your entire package. The balance is typically due a 30 days before your trip begins.
    - ○ Typically, a larger selection of rooms.
    - ○ Bundle park tickets (though it doesn't save you any money this way).
    - ○ You can add flights, transportation, character dining, and tickets to other theme parks.
    - ○ Disneyland.com often has flexible cancellation policies for full refunds.

- Cons:
    - The travel insurance is a lot pricier than most 3rd party sites.
    - You may save money booking with 3rd party sites.

<u>Military Discounts</u> (714-520-7088)

- Military with a valid ID can receive hotel and park ticket discounts:
- Military discounted tickets (saves on 3-day park hopper) – https://disneyland.disney.go.com/offers-discounts/military-3-day-tickets
- Military discounted hotel rooms: https://disneyland.disney.go.com/offers-discounts/military-rooms-discount/

<u>Other great 3rd Party Sites:</u>

Orbitz.com – *highly recommended!*
- Vacation packages available for Disneyland Hotels and other close resorts.
- Promo codes: www.orbitz.com/deals (often 15% off)
- Earn Rewards when you sign up for their discount plan.
- Note: often we find that booking separate hotels on Orbitz.com and a separate flight on Southwest.com are the least expensive options.

Southwest.com
- Often the best deals on flights with 2 free checked bags.
- Southwest offers open seating.
- Tip: If you want to sit next to your friend or family member (especially if you have young children), we highly recommend purchasing the "Early Bird" for $15 each way.

- Flight/Hotel and/or car bundles available at www.SouthwestVacations.com.
- Southwest does not charge fees for changing flights (see their website for details).

Priceline.com
Great hotel selections and vacation packages on an easy to use site. It's hard to find promotional codes for Priceline, but they have great prices.

Purchasing Park Tickets

We recommend saving money by booking tickets early (in case prices go up). The more tickets you purchase, the more you tend to save. Sometimes 3rd-party websites will save you a bit on booking multiday park hopper tickets.

Disneyland.com (714-520-5060)
• Get ticket bundles and more
• Comes with Magic Morning on certain days with a 3-Day ticket. Visit the park early in the morning up to an hour before the park opens.
• Spring Time Multi-Day Discounts for Southern California Residents (March – May).
• Allows you to print tickets, have them mailed, or use your mobile device for eTickets.
• When Disneyland.com has sales, usually the 3rd-party websites will as well.
• Tickets are nonrefundable (if you bundle them with a hotel, they may be refundable).

Southern California CityPASS – a bundled ticket for multiple parks at a large discount.

- Visit www.citypass.com/southern-california to book.
- Parks include:
- Disneyland and Disney California Adventure 3-Day Park Hopper (with Magic Morning)
- SeaWorld
- LEGOLAND California

AAA.com - members save on multi-day tickets and park hoppers.

Annual Passes - The Disneyland Resort offers 4 annual passes to both parks. Passholders receive discounts on dining and merchandise.
1. Disneyland Southern California Select ($329) - Covers about half of the year, but excludes weekends and is exclusive to those living in Southern California.
2. Disneyland California Select ($459) - It's back! More dates, including Sundays and some holidays, that the Californian Select doesn't have.
3. Disney Deluxe Passport ($599) - More days than So Cal Select.
4. Disney Signature Passport ($849) - Most days are available with this pass as well as free parking.
5. Disney Signature Plus Passport ($1,049) - Year-round admission to both parks any day of the year and free parking.

More Information: https://disneyland.disney.go.com/passes

Chapter Six
Traveling to the Resort

Introduction

With the planning out of the way, it's time to being your vacation to the Disneyland Resort. Getting there doesn't have to be tricky, but if you don't plan correctly, it might feel like a mess. Again, we're here to help!

Contrary to what many believe, Disneyland is not in Los Angeles. The Resort is located in Anaheim, California, which is about 25-30 miles south of Los Angeles (a 45-minute drive from the LAX Airport). However, it is easy to travel from Los Angeles to Disneyland and back in a day.

In this chapter, we review the different methods of getting to the resort. How you get there is entirely up to you, but if you're feeling indecisive (or just need more information to choose), read thoroughly to get the best choices.

By Airline

If you aren't planning a road trip and live far away the Disneyland Resort, flying will likely be your best option. While airlines can be expensive at times, we there are several ways to save money:

1. Compare airlines to see the best pricing.

2. Check baggage fees and allowed carry-on items (we like Southwest because they give you 2 free checked bags).

3. Book early to get the best discounts.

Fly into LAX (Los Angeles International):
We recommend LAX because it tends to be the least expensive and easiest to travel from. LAX is located right next to highways that will take you to Disneyland.

By Car

Whether it's a road trip, staying in a neighboring city, or you live close enough to drive to the resort, this can be a great method to take in the beautiful sights of California before you head to the Happiest Place on Earth!

Car Rental: We recommend Enterprise.com or Dollar.com for car rental as they typically have great selection and the best pricing. Pre-booking before you arrive at the airport is advised:

Popular Car Rental Companies:

- www.Enterprise.com: You can visit the company's website or see typically better deals on Priceline.com (or bundle with your airfare and hotel booking).
- www.Dollar.com: click the "specials" tab for deals.
- www.Budget.com: click the "deals" tab for offers.

The Easy Drive to Disneyland from LAX (45 minutes):

1. Follow the signs to I-105 East
2. Take I-105 East to I-5 South
3. Take I-5 South to Disneyland Drive
4. Once on Disneyland Drive, follow the signs to available parking (depending on the time you get to the resort will also depend on which parking is available)
5. Note: We recommend using a GPS navigation app that can help you potentially avoid traffic hotspots. With heavy traffic, this route may not be the best.
6. Note: Sometimes driving to finding parking at the Disneyland Resort can be a bit confusing. Follow the signs as best as you can to ensure that you find parking in a lot or a parking structure.
7. Resort Parking costs $18 (though this can change throughout the year). Parking at Downtown Disney can cost twice as much (if you exceed the hourly limit) and you aren't supposed to park there if you are visiting the parks.
8. Take note of where you parked so that you can easily find your spot again when you leave!

Note: If you've chosen another airport, follow the steps above but I-5 will be your ticket to entering the Disneyland Resort. From San Diego, the northbound carpool lane also empties straight onto Disneyland Drive.

By Shuttle

The Disneyland Resort Express can take you from the airport to Disneyland (LAX and John Wayne Airports only). The shuttle can also drop you off at most of the resort hotels and its surrounding neighbors.

Visit www.graylineanahiem.com to book

- From LAX:
    - $48 *roundtrip/adult*
    - $30 *one way/adult*
- From John Wayne Airport (Orange County):
    - $30 *roundtrip/adult*
    - $20 *one way/adult*
- For each airport, kids under 11 are free with each paying adult. You must order the tickets together for this promotion.
- Look for the Disneyland Express signs in the airport.
- It is highly recommended that you purchase in advance for the best deals and to ensure seating.
- Departures leave throughout the day. Check the website for times before booking.

By Private Car App

With ride-sharing apps like Uber and Lyft taking off, it may seem like a top choice. Both of these services offer private drivers in clean cars (these are not cabs). Here are a few ways you can book:

Uber or Lyft (mobile application):
To download one of these applications, open the App Store (Apple Devices) or Play Store (Android Devices) and search the application by its name.

- These applications will start you at approximately $35-$40 each way (depending on traffic).

- Lyft tends to be less expensive while Uber has a better selection of high-end cars and private options for a premium price.
- Promo codes (typically only for first time riders):

◦ Uber: uber.com/promo (often a free ride)

Notes:
1. Uber doesn't require a tip, and Lyft allows you to. You don't have to tip on these apps and the drivers won't ask you for one.
2. The estimated costs are just that – estimations. The time of day and traffic *does* matter. In the app you can select an estimated fare by entering your destination.

By Train

Taking the train can a be relaxing and beautiful way to travel to the Disneyland Resort. The trains let out at the Anaheim Station and you will need to a second transport from the train station to the resort. The Anaheim Station is 2.5 miles from the Disneyland Resort.

- **Amtrak** – Perfect for longer distances.
  Website: www.Amtrak.com
  Check the "Deals" tab for discounts.
- **Metrolink** – Better pricing for shorter distances (from the south of Anaheim.
  Website: www.metrolinktrains.com

Getting to the Disneyland Resort from the Train Station

- Uber or Lyft – Our most recommended. Fares estimate around $5 each way to the Disneyland Resort (depending on traffic).

By Town Car or Taxi

www.Limos.com- an affordable way to take a private town car, limo, or van for special occasions and large groups.
$10 off promo code from airports: AFF$10.

www.Taxi.com - hail a taxi and ask for a flat rate. These are the typical prices.
- ° LAX: $100 each way
- ° Burbank Airport: $100 each way
- ° Ontario Airport: $100 each way
- ° John Wayne Airport: $45 each way
- ° Long Beach Airport: $45 each way

Note: It is customary to tip your cab driver 15-20%, depending on your experience with the drive.

- Rent a car - Hertz is the closest to the train station. Visit Hertz.com for early booking your car (check the "Discounts & Coupons" tab for deals).

- Taxi - cabs often wait in front of the station. They tend to be a little bit more expensive than Uber or Lyft and you are encouraged to tip.

Chapter Seven
What to Wear and Bring (and What Not to)

Introduction

Now that you've planned your vacation, it's time to figure out what to wear! Luckily, this part is easy (and to experience theme park travelers, it's common knowledge). Disneyland is filled with people from all walks of life, style, and attitude. But everyone is there for the same reason: to have fun at The Happiest Place on Earth! The important thing is to be yourself!

Here we explain how to maximize your fun through comfortable clothing and bringing the right items. Did you know that a bottle of water at the Disneyland Parks can cost $3 or more? In this section, we review tips and tricks for a comfortable and cost-effective stay at the resort.

Note: Be aware that the Disneyland Resort inspects your bags before you enter the parks.

What to Wear and Bring:

1. **Comfortable Clothing** – Shorts, t-shirts, sneakers (trainers), and tank tops are seen all around the parks for a good reason: they are comfortable. You'll be standing in the warm California sun all day, so we recommend that you dress comfortably.

2. **Hats and Sunglasses** – Again, the California sun! It's a wonderful thing, but you don't want to get burned. Be careful of hats and sunglasses on rides (most high-speed attractions will have a compartment to store your items).

3. **Sunscreen** – Even on a cloudy day the ultraviolet rays from the sun can give you an uncomfortable burn. Be careful and stay protected.

4. **Stroller** – Kids can get tired and Disneyland has zones to park these with attendants that watch them while you ride.

5. **A Jacket or Sweater** – Even on a hot day the Disneyland Resort can get chilly at night. We highly recommend having a jacket or sweater to keep you warm.

6. **Water Bottles** – Disneyland will allow you to bring sealed bottles of water into the parks. Save yourself money and bring your own. If you don't mind fountain water, you can refill at water fountains near any restroom for free.

7. **Snacks** – You can save money (or help any picky eaters in your party) by bringing your own snacks.

8. **A Waterproof Cellphone Bag** – If you plan on riding the water attractions like Splash Mountain or Grizzly River

Run, you're likely to get soaked. The last thing you want is to accidently drench your cellphone! Either purchase a waterproof bag (we recommend the FRiEQ case bags that are sold on Amazon.com) or bring a sandwich baggie.

9. **A School-Sized Backpack** – Carry your items in one of these. Make sure it's not too large to fit on the rides. Also keep in mind that your bag will be checked by security before entering the park area.

10. **Money** – The Disneyland Resort accepts all major credit cards and cash. For currency exchange, visit City Hall (Disneyland), Chamber of Commerce (California Adventure), or any resort hotel front desk.

11. **Identification** – For adults, make sure you plan on bringing your government-issued ID if you plan to drink alcoholic beverages.

12. **Rainy Days** – It doesn't rain much at the Disneyland Resort (only around 12 inches of rainfall in a year), but just in case it does, here's what to bring:
    a. Compact Umbrella – On rainy days, this is very handy. Don't bring a full sized umbrella, as it won't fit on rides and will be difficult to carry around.
    b. Poncho – It might be a bit of a fashion *faux pas* to some, but a poncho could keep you and your belongings dry. Many visitors love wearing these for the water rides as well!

Note:
For information about what to bring for babies and toddlers, please see our Family with Kids Guide (Chapter 13).

What *Not* to Wear or Bring:

1. **Selfie Sticks** - It seems like it would be so much fun, but Disneyland bans them for the safety of other guests.

2. **Adult Costumes and Masks** - children under 14 are allowed to wear costumes, but as not to trick people into think a non-cast member is a character, Disneyland bans these for adults. During Mickey's Halloween Party, you may dress in costume.

3. **Skateboards, Rollerblades, Bikes, Roller skates** - Disneyland bans these for safety reasons. Even those skates that slide out from kids' shoes are banned. If you need a vehicle, you may rent a scooter or wheelchair from Guest Services to the right of the Disneyland entrance gates.

4. **Remote Control Toys and Drones** - Sorry, but not allowed.

5. **Your Pet** - If you need to place for your dog or cat during your stay, the Disneyland Resort Kennel Club offers daily service for $20 per pet. Keep in mind that you will need to feed your pet during the day and they don't provide overnight packages. Call (714) 781-7662 for details. Service animals, however, are allowed inside the parks.
   If you need overnight accommodations for your dog, Camp Bow Wow is about 15 minutes from the resort: campbowwow.com/anaheim or call (714) 533-2267.

6. **Alcoholic Beverages** - These are not allowed in the parks (though you may purchase alcoholic drinks at Disney California Adventure and Downtown Disney).

7. **Lawn Chairs** - You might be tempted to bring these to watch a parade, but Disneyland bans them. We assume it's to keep the resort's aesthetics away from looking like a 4th of July picnic.

8. **Glass Bottles** - Another safety precaution. However, small glass containers of baby food are allowed.

9. **Bags with Wheels and Hiking Backpacks**

10. **Wrapped Gifts** - For inspection reasons, you cannot bring wrapped gifts into the park. If you plan on giving someone a present, choose a gift bag or wrap it when you get to the park.

Backup Plans

Rent a Locker - We suggest renting a locker to everyone. There's no need to tire yourself out with a hefty backpack when a locker that fits your belongings starts at just $7 for a day rental (yes, night is included, too).
- Lockers are located just outside of each park gate
- Inside the park, lockers are to the right:
    - Disneyland - Main Street
    - California Adventure - Buena Vista Street

Plan a Midday Return to Your Hotel - If you don't want to rent a locker, make a plan to return to your hotel midday. There you can eat, refill on drinks, and maybe take a power nap. When you're refreshed, head back to the parks for more fun!
★ **Magic Tip** ★
If you forget any of these items, Disneyland sells them. Check the Main Street, U.S.A., Buena Vista Street, and Downtown Disney shops for any items that you may need.

Chapter Eight
Hotel Guide

Introduction

As you near the property of the Disneyland Resort, one of the first things you'll notice are the collections of hotels near the entrance. The City of Anaheim has a bit of a mid-century charm set in suburbia (and is heavily influenced by the parks), and the hotels reflect this appeal.

Since there are so many hotels, inns, and motels, it may be very difficult for you to choose where to stay. Ultimately, the choice comes down to staying on or off the resort – followed by *which* hotel to reserve your room with.

In this section, we outline the pros and cons of staying off and on the Disneyland Resort. We give you our recommendations, hotel details, and tips for saving on booking to help you make your decision with ease.

Should I Stay On or Off the Disneyland Resort?

The Disneyland Resort offers three amazing hotels, each with a different theme. The most luxurious is Disney's Grand Californian Hotel and Spa, followed by the classic Disneyland Hotel, and the more affordable Disney's Paradise Pier Hotel. However, none of these properties run cheap. Since they have exclusive access to the parks, extended park hours, and many more surprises, we recommend staying on resort property.

However, it's not necessary to stay on property. Many more affordable hotels are within walking distance of the resort. These properties may offer nice rooms, pools, breakfast, and sometimes a views of Disneyland from your room. All of this while potentially saving you hundreds of dollars (or *thousands*, depending on your length of stay).

Tips for Booking Discounts on Hotels:

1. When you book online at Disneyland.com or over the phone, you can often just put $200 down on a reservation (this includes any bundled park tickets and added items) and pay the remaining balance closer to your arrival date.

2. Always check 3rd party travel websites for better deals (i.e.: Orbitz.com, Bookit.com, Expedia.com) and compare to the Disneyland website.

3. Sometimes you can save quite a bit per night with third-party websites. Click on their "deals" or "promotions" tab

to find discount coupons on the sites (we outlined our most recommended previously in Chapter 5).

4. Though many websites offer packaged deals, sometimes these are not the lowest cost. We recommend checking the pricing of hotels and flights separately before you commit to a vacation package.

5. Seasonally, Disneyland.com will offer discounted hotel pricing (sometimes 30% off or more). We recommended booking early when you see these deals!

Disneyland® Resort Properties

There are three hotel properties on the resort, each with their own unique sense of themed magic from a wilderness lodge to a beachside hotel. There's something for everyone here, but sometimes it's hard to decide since each has its perks, whether it's the amenities, the views, or the overcall cost.

Benefits of Staying at a Disneyland Resort Hotel:
1. Closest proximity to the parks (save on walking time).
2. "Extra Magic Hours" get hotel guests in the park earlier (or later) than anyone else on select dates.
3. Private entrance for guests of all 3 hotels through the Grand Californian Hotel to Disney California Adventure.
4. Walking distance to the restaurants, shops, and fun of Downtown Disney.
5. Free merchandise delivery to your hotel from any of the Disney shops in the parks. The following day you can pick them up from the bell services in your hotel.
6. Gorgeous pools with waterslides.

7. Disney Character Wake-Up Calls from one of your favorites.
8. Free Wi-Fi.

The Disneyland Hotel Overview

1150 Magic Way, Anaheim, CA 92802
Booking: www.Disneyland.com or call (714) 778-6600

Star Rating: 4

The Disneyland Hotel is our top choice because of its pure-Disney appeal and location at the end of Downtown Disney. Opened in 1955, every piece from the lobby design to the hotel décor, you instantly immersed in Walt Disney's magic.

Pros:

- Elegantly designed rooms and suites that bring Disney and mid-century elegance seamlessly together.

- Large pool with two monorail-themed water slides and the smaller D-Ticket pool.

- Trader Sam's Enchanted Tiki Bar with top-notch cocktails and American bar food. For those wishing that Disneyland® had a bar, this is what you've been looking for! When you order special drinks, the entire bar changes, erupting with volcanoes or thunder and lightning – they don't call Trader Sam's an "enchanted" tiki bar for nothing!

- E-Ticket Club-Level option available with continental breakfast, sodas, snacks, desserts, evening wine and cheese, and more. You can even view the fireworks display from the club room.

- Typically, less expensive than the Grand Californian. We also like the design of the Disneyland Hotel standard rooms more than we do the Grand Californian standard rooms.

- Close to Downtown Disney attractions, restaurants, and shopping.

Cons:
° Further than the Grand Californian. Since the Disneyland Hotel is located at the opposite end of Downtown Disney from the theme parks, it may be a little of bit of a pain walking there. However, the monorail is always a fast solution that departs out of Tomorrowland to the Disneyland Hotel.

° The Disneyland Hotel is a premium destination that comes with a premium price. A less expensive alternative would be the Paradise Pier Hotel or a hotel outside of the resort.

Disney's Grand Californian Hotel and Spa

1600 Disneyland Dr., Anaheim, CA 92802
Booking: www.Disneyland.com or call (714) 778-6600

Star Rating: 4

A visitor favorite, Disney's Grand Californian brings luxury to the Disneyland Resort. The hotel opened just before Disney California Adventure in 2001 and is designed after hotels in Northern California (if you've ever been to the Ahwahnee Hotel in Yosemite, it has a similar magnificent appeal).

Pros:

- It's beautiful! Hotel guest will be stunned when entering the grand lobby of this magnificent hotel.

- The closest hotel to the resort with a private entrance to the Disney California Adventure for its guest. This is our favorite feature, especially since the entrance is by the Grizzly River Run, so it makes a great stopping point if you need to change after getting soaked!

- Classily designed rooms and suites with a lodge feel.

- Three pools: The Fountain Pool, Redwood Pool with water slide, and the Mariposa Pool for relaxing. Poolside Cabanas available at the Mariposa Pool.

- Spa that offers massages, facials, and other treatments.

- Close to Downtown Disney attractions, restaurants, and shopping.

Cons:

- The Grand Californian is a luxury destination that comes with a luxury price. It is often the most expensive of three Disneyland Resort hotels.

- The standard rooms as missing some of the classic appeal found in the artwork and details of the Disneyland Hotel rooms.

Disney's Paradise Pier Hotel

1717 Disneyland Dr., Anaheim, CA 92802
Booking: www.Disneyland.com or call (714) 778-6600

Star Rating: 4

The Paradise Pier may be the lowest priced hotel on the resort, but it's still a premium stay with splendid rooms. In fact, Paradise Pier has generally the largest room sizes of any of the resorts. Many families with children enjoy staying here because of the low cost and extra square footage.

Pros:

- Stylishly designed rooms and suites themed as a 1920s beachfront hotel.
- The lowest price of the three resort hotels.
- Typically, the largest rooms of the three resort hotels.
- Rooftop pools with the Paradise Spa whirlpool, a children's pool, and a waterslide in the Paradise Pool.
- The Surfside Lounge serves up cocktails for adults 21 and up.

- Close to Downtown Disney attractions, restaurants, and shopping.
- See the fireworks from the pool deck on select nights.

Cons:

- The furthest hotel in the resort from the parks. Disney's Paradise Pier Hotel is still close to the end of Downtown Disney and near the Disneyland. Therefore, the walking distance from the theme parks to the hotel might be a bit of a trek. To avoid this, we recommend taking the monorail out of Tomorrowland to the Disneyland Hotel. The Paradise Pier is just a short walking distance away from there.
- The hotel is missing some of the magic felt in the other two resort hotels. The Paradise Pier Hotel feels more like a standard hotel without the grandiose lobbies. However, the rooms don't disappoint Disney lovers with their themed décor.

Even Mores Reasons to Stay at a Disneyland Resort Hotel:

Hotel Parking: You still have to pay for this but the parking is much closer than the rest of the resort and you can leave your vehicle overnight (check Disneyland.com for details on cars and oversized vehicles as they are subject to change). Valet is also available at an additional cost.

Power Walks through Disneyland are offered to hotel guests beginning at 6AM. Check with the Guest Services Desk at your resort hotel for details.

Breakfast with Disney Characters: Fun for the kid in all of us and delicious food from eggs and bacon to pancakes and fresh-made omelets. Locations are as follows:
- Disneyland Hotel: Goofy's Kitchen
- Grand Californian: Storyteller's Café
- Paradise Pier: PCH Grill

★ **Magic Tip** ★
Check Disneyland.com for dining times and to reserve your spot early. You do not have to be a guest at the hotel to dine with the characters.

Laundry: You may have your clothes dry cleaned or laundered Monday through Saturday. Perfect for those traveling long, staying extendedly, or stopping by during a business trip. The Grand Californian has its own laundry room for self-service.

Hotel Dining

Disneyland Hotel

Restaurants

<u>Goofy's Kitchen</u> – *Top Choice!*
Description: American Breakfast and Dinner with buffet options.
Type: Table Service (Breakfast and Dinner)
Age Group: Everyone
Price: $$$$
Adult Beverages: Yes
Reservations: Disneyland.com or (714) 781-3463

Recommendation:
> Breakfast: Brunch Buffet
> Dinner: Dinner Buffet

Steakhouse 55
Description: Elegant American Steakhouse
Type: Table Service (Breakfast and Dinner)
Age Group: Everyone
Price: $$$$
Adult Beverages: Yes
Reservations: Disneyland.com or (714) 781-3463
Recommendation:
> Starter: Maryland Crab Cake
> Entrée: the steaks here are delicious!

Tangaroa Terrace
Description: American and Polynesian Cuisine
Type: Fast Service (Breakfast, Lunch, and Dinner)
Price: $$
Age Group: Everyone
Adult Beverages: Yes
Reservations: Disneyland.com or (714) 781-3463
Recommendation:
> Breakfast: French Toast (with banana-caramel sauce)
> Lunch or Dinner: Angus Hawaiian Cheeseburger

Bars and Lounges

Trader Sam's Enchanted Tiki Bar – *Top Choice!*
Description: located by the Disneyland Hotel Pool, this authentic Disney "dive bar" serves American food with a full bar. Volcanos erupt and storms brew inside of the room with the order of certain drinks. We never thought that Disneyland would make a dive bar,

but we are so glad that they did! Trader Sam's is fun for everyone (though it becomes 21 and over after 8pm).
Type: "Dive Bar" and Lounge
Age Group: Adult (though there are options for kids)
Price: $$
Adult Beverages: Yes (full bar and cocktails)
Reservations: None
Recommendations:
>Cocktails: The Uh Oa! (rum blends with passion fruit), Krakatoa Punch (rum punch), and Ka-blue-ie! (tropical rum with blue curacao) are our personal favorites.
>Eats: The Angus Hawaiian Cheeseburger or Chicken Lettuce Wraps.

★ **Magic Tips** ★
1. "Adult Dole Whip" - this is a secret menu item for those who love the tropical-flavored drinks. The concoction is made with rum, pineapple juice, and some other things we can't place. It's recommended that you sit at the bar and get friendly with a bartender to ask for the drink. Not every bartender there will know how to make it.
2. Trader Sam's doesn't list their drink prices, but they are often anywhere from $10 - $30 (the higher priced drinks are the ones that make the room erupt or storm).

The Lounge at Steakhouse 55
Description: The bar at Steakhouse 55 restaurant
Type: Elegant Bar and Lounge
Age Group: Adult
Price: $$
Adult Beverages: Yes (full bar and cocktails)
Reservations: None
Recommendations:
>Cocktails: Any! They are all fantastic choices.
>Eats: Main Lobster Roll Sliders.

Disney Grand Californian Resort and Spa

Restaurants

Storytellers Café – *Top Choice!*
Description: American Breakfast, Lunch, and Dinner with buffet options.
Type: Table Service (and Character Breakfast)
Age Group: Everyone
Price: Breakfast and Dinner $$$$ (Lunch $$$)
Adult Beverages: Yes (Lunch and Dinner)
Reservations: Disneyland.com or (714) 781-3463
Recommendation:
    Breakfast: Brunch Buffet
    Lunch: Slow-roasted Turkey Clubhouse
    Dinner: Dinner Buffet

Napa Rose
Description: California-themed Upscale Dining with entrées designed by gourmet Napa chef, Andrew Sutton.
Type: Dinner
Age Group: Adult (though there are options for kids)
Price: $$$$
Adult Beverages: Yes (great wine selection)
Reservations: Disneyland.com or (714) 781-3463
Recommendation:
    Starter: Roasted Breast of Pheasant with Duck Liver Mousseline
    Lunch: Any of the main courses as they were all designed by gourmet Chef Andrew Sutton.
    Dinner: Dinner Buffet

Bars and Lounges

Napa Rose Lounge
Description: The bar lounge inside of the Napa Rose (more casual than Napa Rose).
Type: Lounge
Age Group: Adult
Price: $$
Adult Beverages: Yes (full bar, wine, and cocktails)
Reservations: None
Recommendations:
>Wine: Domaine Chandon, Etoile, Brut Rose (Californian Sparkling Rose)
>Cocktails: Moscow Mule (vodka, lime, ginger beer in a copper mug)
>Eats: The wood-fired Pizzetta of the Season or Wine County Pheasant Meatloaf

Hearthstone Lounge
Description: a bar lounge
Type: Lounge (lobby)
Price: $$
Age Group: Adult
Adult Beverages: Yes (wine, beer, and cocktails)
Reservations: None
Recommendations:
>Wine and Cocktails: see "Napa Rose Lounge
>Eats: Two Mini Wagyu Sliders (served with skinny fries)

Disney Paradise Pier Hotel

Restaurants

Disney's PCH Grill –*Great Choice!*
Description: American Buffet Breakfast and Dinner with Buffet Options.
Type: Table Service (and Character Breakfast)
Age Group: Everyone
Price: Breakfast and Dinner $$$
Adult Beverages: None
Reservations: Disneyland.com or (714) 781-3463
Recommendation:
    Breakfast: Brunch Buffet
    Dinner: Dinner Buffet

Bars and Lounges

Surfside Lounge
Description: California beach-themed bar and lounge
Type: Lounge (Breakfast snacks, full lunch and dinner)
Age Group: Everyone
Price: $$
Adult Beverages: Yes (full bar, wine, and cocktails)
Reservations: None
Recommendations:
    Breakfast: "Mickey" Waffles
    Appetizer: beer-battered Onion Rings or Monterey Bay Spinach and Artichoke Dip
    Lunch/Dinner: Paradise Pier Club (turkey club)

<u>The Sand Bar</u>
Description: California beach-themed bar near the lobby
Type: Lounge (drinks and sandwiches)
Age Group: Adult
Price: $$
Adult Beverages: Yes (full bar, wine, and cocktails)
Reservations: None

More Ideas (all hotels)

- Order In-Room Service from a menu located in your hotel room.
- Visit the Coffee House for sandwiches, pastries, and, of course, coffee.
- Head to Downtown Disney for Starbucks and many other eateries.

Recommended Properties Outside of the Resort:

For those looking to save money, staying at the Disneyland Resort Hotels may not be an option. The good news is there are several hotels nearby that offer transportation or are within walking distance.

Here are the places we that recommend:

1. **Courtyard Marriott Anaheim Theme Park Entrance**
   Star Rating: 3
   Price: Moderate
   Distance: 5-minute walk to the Disneyland Resort

Pool: Yes
Perks: Close to the theme parks, pool with waterslides, certain rooms have resort views
Contact: (714) 254-1442 / www.marriott.com

2. **The Anabella**
   Star Rating: 3
   Price: Moderate
   Distance: 5-minute walk to the Disneyland Resort
   Pool: Yes
   Perks: Classic hotel at a great price, certain rooms have resort views
   Contact: (800) 863-4888 / www.anabellahotel.com (check the promotions tab for deals)

3. **Hyatt Regency Orange County**
   Star Rating: 4
   Price: Moderate
   Distance: 1 mile walk to the Disneyland Resort / also offers shuttles for $5 each adult
   Pool: Yes (2)
   Perks: Beautiful, premium hotel near the convention center
   Contact: (714) 750-1234 / orangecounty.hyatt.com (click the "offers" tab for deals)

4. **Candy Cane Inn**
   Star Rating: 2
   Price: Economic
   Distance: ½ mile (under 10 minute) walk to the Disneyland Resort
   Pool: Yes (2)
   Perks: Classic inn feel with free breakfast and coffee
   Contact: (714) 774-5284 / www.candycaneinn.net (check the website for promo codes)

5. **Del Sol Inn**
   Star Rating: 2
   Price: Economic
   Distance: 5-minute walk to the Disneyland Resort
   Pool: Yes
   Perks: Classic inn feel that is very close to the resorts
   Contact: (888) 686-1122 / www.delsolinn.com (click the promotions tab for deals)

Chapter Nine
Disneyland

Introduction

When we know that a friend or family member is going to visit Disneyland, we become excited for them. We love offering tips and ideas for attractions to make their visit even better.

Disneyland is the original world-class theme park that opened its gates over 60 years ago, in July of 1955. With more than 60 rides and attractions across 8 lands (Main Street, U.S.A., Adventureland, Frontierland, New Orleans Square, Critter Country, Fantasyland, Mickey's Toontown, and Tomorrowland) the Disneyland Park has something for everyone.

In this section, we will review the magical park that started it all! Disneyland has an undeniable charm that will come over you, bringing you into the wonderful world of Walt Disney.

Note: Please be sure to read the **Magic Tips** in this section. They are designed to help you avoid long lines and bring fun activities in focus. Follow these and they will make your time at the Disneyland Park even more enjoyable.

Main Street, U.S.A.

Disneyland's iconic grand entrance filled with shops, dining, and a magnificent view of the castle. The first thing you'll notice is the train station, beautiful flower arrangements, and smiling faces. Choose the left or the right side of the entrance to find yourself in a hub of horse-drawn street cars, carriages, unique shops, and Disney characters waiting to greet you. At night, Main Street U.S.A. becomes the center for the Paint the Night Parade and the Disneyland fireworks show.

Theme: Turn-of-the-century American town (specifically, Walt Disney's hometown of Marceline, Missouri in the early 20th century).

★ Magic Tips ★

1. Main Street makes a great viewing spot for many of the parades and nighttime fireworks displays. Crowds line up along the streets typically 30 minutes before each show to get a great view. If you'd like to avoid the parades and shows, it's best to stay clear of Main Street around the show times.
2. Get souvenirs here on your way out of the park. They have everything from character antennae balls to clothing to candy.
3. Rent a locker here if you need space to store your things (they start at $7 for rental the entire day). Lockers are located behind the fruit stand on the right side as you walk toward the castle.
4. For Disneyland Resort hotel guests, Main Street, U.S.A. often opens an hour earlier (Extra Magic Hour) than the rest of the park.

Rides

Main Street Vehicles
Description: Ride a horse-drawn streetcar, horseless carriage, or a double-decker bus that will take you down to Sleeping Beauty Castle.
Level: Family
Recommendation: A nice stroll for small children and guests who enjoy the classic appeal of Disney attractions. However, thrill riders might rather skip this and head straight to a ride like Space Mountain.
FastPass: None

Disneyland Railroad – Down for refurbishment until Summer 2017
Description: a railroad that moves around the perimeter of the park and makes stops in New Orleans Square, Fantasyland/Toontown, and Tomorrowland.
Level: Everyone

Recommendation: Fun if you'd like an easy way to ride from town to town. If you take the railroad all around the perimeter of the park, you will see surprises like volcanoes and dinosaurs!
FastPass: None

Shows and Attractions:

<u>Paint the Night</u> (Disneyland – Returns Summer 2017)
A vibrant new nighttime parade starring favorite characters from Mickey to Tinker Bell! The spinning lights will catch the eye of everyone around in this state-of-the-art attraction.

Get Preferred Viewing (and beat the crowds):
- Book a reservation at Aladdin's Oasis and receive an "on-the-go" meal as well as preferred seating to Paint the Night.
- To book, visit Disneyland.com or call (714) 781-4565 up to 60 days in advance.

★ Magic Tips ★
The parade route curls at the end of Main Street, U.S.A. and we recommend this as a viewing area. The Disneyland Fireworks show typically follows shortly after Paint the Night. Main Street often closes an hour after the park closes.

<u>"Fantasy In the Sky"</u> **Fireworks (Disneyland)**
Disneyland's stunning classic fireworks display. Watch the magic all around the park as fireworks set off behind Sleeping Beauty Castle.

★ Magic Tips ★
- The best viewing is on Main Street, U.S.A. as the projections light up the buildings all around you. It's recommended that you watch the Main Street Electrical Parade or Paint the Night

Parade first and wait for the Disneyland fireworks minutes later.
- The fireworks go off behind the castle, so the closer you are to the castle, the larger they will appear.
- If you are staying the Disneyland Hotel or the Paradise Pier, they offer special rooftop firework viewing from the property. This is especially great if you wish to avoid the crowds.
- Staying at the Grand Californian? Ask the concierge how you can enjoy private hotel firework shows.

The Disneyland Story presenting Great Moments with Mr. Lincoln
Description: An animatronic show starring President Abraham Lincoln.
Level: Everyone
Recommendation: Perfect for guests who love the nostalgia of Disneyland. However, this classic attraction can feel very dated. Thrill-seekers and children will likely want to skip this one for this reason.
FastPass: None

Main Street Electrical Parade (Only until Summer 2017)
Description: A classic light-up nighttime parade
Level: Family
Recommendation: Designed for those looking for a classic Disneyland Parade. The Main Street Electrical Parade ends its final run where it originally began, at Disneyland.
FastPass: None

Even More:
You can also discover the many shops, City Hall, the Main Street Cinema playing classic Disney Studio animated shorts, and the Disneyland Gallery.

Restaurants and Eateries

The Carnation Café®
Description: Early 20th-century American café with classic.
Type: Table-service
Age Group: Everyone
Pricing: $$
Recommendation: The breakfast here is quite good, and the Main Street Cheeseburger, Sourdough Bacon-Cheese Melt, and Green Chili Burger are delicious for lunch. If you enjoy coffee, we recommend ordering a cup with the Mickey Mouse souvenir mug. The Carnation Café also has amazing malts.

Market House (Starbucks)
Description: Yep, even Disneyland has a Starbucks!
Type: Coffee Shop
Age Group: Adults
Pricing: $
Recommendation: The lines can be somewhat long in the morning, but they are quick to service everyone.
Tip: It might be a little hard to find the Market House sign, but it is right across from the Carnation Café, on your right as you walk toward the castle.

Plaza Inn®
Description: A classic, wonderfully detailed restaurant on the corner of Main Street and Tomorrowland.
Type: Table-service with character buffet
Age Group: Everyone
Pricing: $$
Recommendation: The fried chicken is famous here. You can also have breakfast with Minnie and her friends.

More Eateries (Pricing: $)

Gibson Girl Ice Cream Parlor – Serving up Disneyland's scrumptious ice cream. Get it in a waffle cone.
Refreshment Corner – Get a Coke soft drink or, better yet, a famous chili dog here.
Jolly Holiday Bakery Café – *Mary Poppins*-themed fresh bakery with delicious treats, coffee, and tea.

Adventureland

Theme: Enter the jungle, explore ruins, and ride the Indiana Jones Adventure in this lush and beautifully landscaped attraction area.

★ Magic Tips ★
1. The shops across from the Jungle Cruise sell Indiana Jones merchandise including his famous hat.
2. If you're running short on time and want to eat, the Bengal Barbecue has quick-order kabobs to take on the go.

Rides

Indiana Jones™ Adventure
Description: travel through a hidden jungle temple and hop aboard a classic jeep-like vehicle that holds up to 12 passengers.
Level: Thrill Ride (must be 46"/117cm or taller)
Recommendation: This is a unique ride that is only at Disneyland and it should not be missed by thrill riders.
FastPass: Available to the left of the entrance.
★ Magic Tips ★
1. On a crowded day, ask the cast member at the entrance of the ride (typically dressed like Indiana Jones) about the

"Single Rider Line" - you will receive a pass to cut through the bulk of the line and you will likely not sit with the rest of your party when boarding. Sometimes this option is not faster, though is usually is.
2. This ride is similar to the Dinosaur ride at Disney World's Animal Kingdom, but a lot more thrilling with special effects, twists, and turns.
3. There are many different chambers to start with either eternal youth, riches, or knowledge. However, the ride after that feels generally the same as it rides along the same track afterward.
4. In the spike chamber in the queue, look for a bamboo pole. Shake it until you hear the room rumble and the spikes fall from above.
5. Look for a "don't pull the rope" sign in the queue above the well. Do it and hear the person below yell for help!

Jungle Cruise

Description: Venture down a massive river on a boat with your tour comedic tour guide. See animatronic Amazonian and African animals from monkeys and crocodiles to elephants and lions on this 7-minute long ride.
Level: Everyone
Recommendation: A classic, humorous Disneyland ride that most guests will enjoy. Thrill riders may want to skip it.
FastPass: None
* Magic Tips *
1. The holiday version, Jingle Cruise (November – December) offers Christmas lights, a different script, and animals wearing Christmas hats.

Tarzan's Treehouse™

Description: Climbable treehouse themed after Disney's Tarzan animated film. This attraction once was the Swiss Family Robinson Treehouse.

Level: Young Kids / Everyone
Recommendation: Kids ages 10 and under will love this attraction that typically has a very short line (or no wait at all).
FastPass: None
★ **Magic Tips** ★
1. One of the best photo opportunities is here. Climb to the top and take a photo at the top for something stunning to share.

Shows and Attractions

Enchanted Tiki Room
Description: An animatronic show starring birds and Tikis in a tropical island setting.
Level: Family / Everyone
Recommendation: Have a Dole® Whip while you watch the 15-minute long show. Thrill-seekers will want to skip this one, as it's a classic attraction that can feel a bit dated.
FastPass: None

Aladdin's Oasis
Description: *Aladdin*-themed show and "On-The-Go" meals.
Type: "On-The-Go" service (take the meal with you)
Price: $$
Recommendation: Lasagna Bolognese
★ **Magic Tip** ★
You can get the best viewing for the Paint the Night Parade when eating at Aladdin's Oasis. Visit Disneyland.com (or call 714-781-DINE) to book your reservation up to 60 days in advance.

Restaurants and Eateries

Bengal Barbecue
Description: South Asian style barbecue serving coffee drinks, soda pops, and delicious kabobs.
Type: Fast service
Age Group: Adults (no kids' menu)
Price: $$
Recommendation: The Bengal Beef Skewer or the Outback Vegetable Skewer.

Tiki Juice Bar (hosted by Dole®) – *Top Choice!*
Description: Juice bar serving the famous Disneyland Dole® Whip.
Type: Fast Service stand
Age Group: Everyone
Price: $
Recommendation: the pineapple-flavored Dole Whip floats are one of Disneyland's most famous recipes and our top treat recommendation.
★ **Magic Tip** ★ The line may be long, but it's worth it. However, in the summer, we've seen the line nearly an hour during the hottest parts of the day. It may be wise to come back when the day has cooled along with the line.

Frontierland

Theme: Immerse yourself in the wild west near the Rivers of America. Ride the high-speed Big Thunder Mountain Railroad or catch a lighthearted show at the Golden Horseshoe Stage.

Rides

Big Thunder Mountain Railroad
Description: A fast rollercoaster with few dips called "The Wildest Ride in the Wilderness"
Level: Thrill Ride (must be 40"/102cm or taller)
Recommendation: Many families and thrill riders will love this fast rollercoaster with short dips and great special effects.
FastPass: Available near the entrance.

Also See:
• **Mark Twain Riverboat** - Explore a beautiful American-style riverboat.
• **Frontierland Shootin' Exposition** - A paid experience where you can shoot targets with laser-guided rifles.

Closed for refurbishment until Summer 2017:

- **Pirate's Lair on Tom Sawyer Island** – board a raft and set sail for an island playground perfect for Kids and Tweens.
- **Sailing Ship Columbia** – a massive 18th-century themed boat that sails guest around the Rivers of America.
- **Davy Crockett's Explorer Canoes** – don't come with your arms sore! Guests paddle down the Rivers of American in Frontierland while seeing the stunning waterscape of Disneyland.

Shows and Attractions

The Golden Horseshoe Stage
Description: A family-friendly saloon-style show and dining experience.
Level: Family / Everyone
Recommendation: Western-style show with songs and jokes while you dine. Walt Disney himself loved this attraction!
FastPass: None

Restaurants and Eateries

The Golden Horseshoe
Description: Western dining experience with American fare
Type: Fast service
Age Group: Everyone
Price: $$
Recommendation: Chili in a Bread Bowl

River Belle Terrace
Description: western dining experience with American fare
Type: Fast service

Age Group: Everyone
Price: $$
Recommendation: Pork Spareribs or River Belle's Chopped Salad

<u>Stage Door Café</u>
Description: Western dining experience with American favorites
Age Group: Everyone
Type: Fast service
Price: $
Recommendation: Hand-dipped corn dog

<u>Rancho del Zocalo Restaurante</u>
Description: Mexican food
Type: Fast service
Age Group: Everyone
Price: $$
Recommendation: Mickey Mouse Pancake for Breakfast or Citrus Fire-grilled Chicken or Burrito Guadalajara for lunch/dinner.
★ Magic Tips ★
The pumpkin flan during Halloween (mid-September – October) and Tres Leche Cake at the Holiday time (November – December) are fan favorite desserts!

New Orleans Square

Theme: A southern America-themed land filed with shops, treats, and a couple of very famous rides including Pirates of the Caribbean and the Haunted Mansion. Dine on creole favorites or catch a different angle of the nighttime spectacular "Fantasy In The Sky" over the Rivers of America.

Rides

Pirates of the Caribbean
Description: Pirate-themed boat ride in the dark
Level: Everyone
Recommendation: Both thrill riders and families will love this attraction.
FastPass: None
★ Magic Tips ★
1. When facing the entrance, the line on the right is typically the shortest (there is less queue than the left side).
2. A great air conditioned ride to cool off on warm days.

Haunted Mansion
Description: A slow-paced ride through a haunted house.
Level: Everyone (though young children may become frightened)
Recommendation: It's a Disneyland classic that many thrill-riders may want to skip for it's slow movement and effects that are only scary enough to terrify young children. However, if it's in the Holiday season (mid-September through December), we highly recommend the Haunted Mansion Holiday (themed after Tim Burton's *The Nightmare Before Christmas*), with added special effects and animatronics.
FastPass: Available near the entrance

Shows and Attractions

Fantasmic! (Returns Summer 2017)
Description: A stunning nighttime show starring Mickey and ending with the famous dragon from Sleeping Beauty.
Level: Family / Everyone
Recommendation: A perfect nighttime spectacular for show fans.
FastPass: Yes

★ Magic Tip ★
Get a FastPass for Fantasmic! at the start of your day. This won't prevent you from getting other FastPasses as it is "disconnected" from the rest.

Restaurants and Eateries

Blue Bayou Restaurant
Description: Disneyland's premier dining experience with some of the best entrees the Disneyland Resort has to offer. Located inside of the Pirates of the Caribbean ride, this is exceptional Louisiana-style dining with creole food and more. Even in the middle of the day, you will feel as though you are dining next to a Louisiana Bayou at night!
Type: Table service
Age Group: Everyone (teenagers and adults will especially love this restaurant)
Price: $$$$
Recommendations:
1. *Le Special de* Monte Cristo Sandwich is our absolute favorite entrée in the entire resort!
    a. The Monte Cristo is a battered and fried sandwich filled with ham, turkey, and Swiss cheese. To top it off, there are dipping sauces (berry jam and a sweet crème), plus the sandwich is dusted with powder sugar. We know it sounds odd to newbies, but it's an absolute delight and worth trying!
    b. This is a lot of food for most people (the large sandwich comes in four pieces). You can always split the entrée to save money as the meal also comes with a side salad and fruit skewer.
    c. The Monte Cristo is *only* served at lunch.

2. Louisiana Lemonade – Lemonade and Sprite® and mango/raspberry blends poured over a glowing ice cube (that you can keep).

★ **Magic Tips** ★
1. Book your reservation EARLY for the Blue Bayou on Disneyland.com (or call 714-781-DINE). You can book up to 60 days in advance.
2. If you can't get a reservation at all, check Café Orleans as they tend have more availability and a similar menu with outdoor seating.

Café Orleans

Description: French-style soups, sandwiches, crepes, and salads in the center of New Orleans Square. This is a great alternative to the Blue Bayou with outdoor seating and views of the Rivers of America.

Type: Table service
Age Group: Everyone
Price: $$$

Recommendation: Monte Cristo Sandwich (see Blue Bayou description above), Three-Cheese Monte Cristo, New Orleans Gumbo, or Chicken Gumbo Crepe.

★ **Magic Tip** ★
1. We also recommend booking in advance at Disneyland.com (or call 714-781-DINE). You can book up to 60 days in advance.

French Market Restaurant

Description: French-style soups, sandwiches, crepes, and salads in the center of New Orleans Square. This is a great alternative to the Blue Bayou with outdoor seating and views of the Rivers of America.

Type: Fast Service
Age Group: Everyone
Price: $$

Recommendation: French Dip Sandwich or Creamy Corn Chowder (served in a bread bowl)

French Market Restaurant
Description: French-style eats
Type: Fast service
Age Group: Everyone
Price: $$
Recommendation: French Dip Sandwich

Royal Street Veranda
Description: French-style soups
Type: Fast service
Age Group: Adults and Teenagers
Price: $$
Recommendation: Creamy Clam Chowder (served in a sourdough bread bowl).

Also recommended

Mint Julep Bar ($) – Mickey-shaped beignets, lattes, mochas, and, of course, mint juleps.

Critter Country

Theme: A backwoods and forest-themed land, home of Splash Mountain.

Rides:
Splash Mountain
Description: Water-based log ride starring the singing critters from *Song of the South*

Level: Thrill (must be 40"/102cm or taller)
Recommendation: If you love getting wet and drops, this is the ride for you!
FastPass: Available
★ Magic Tips ★
1. This ride typically has the longest lines, especially during the hotter days. A FastPass is recommended.
2. Sit near the back to avoid getting as wet (though you will still likely get wet). Ask a cast member at the end of the line to sit in the back and they will help accommodate you.
3. If you want to get soaked – ask a cast member to sit in the front!
4. If it's a cold day or you just don't feel like getting your clothes wet, either buy/bring a poncho or skip this attraction (though it is one of our favorites).
5. Say cheese! The camera for Splash Mountain is on the left side of the boat as you plunge down the last drop.

The Many Adventures of Winnie the Pooh
Description: A slow-paced ride through the brightly-colored world of Winnie the Pooh.
Level: Young Kids / Family
Recommendation: Great for small kids, but teens and thrill-riders will want to skip.
FastPass: None

Restaurants and Eateries

Hungry Bear Restaurant
Description: Picnic-style sandwiches, burgers, and fries
Type: Fast service
Age Group: Everyone (many kids' choices)

Price: $
Recommendation: Turkey Caesar Wrap and Onion Rings
★ **Magic Tips** ★
1. There is quieter seating here by the Rivers of America. After ordering your food, walk to the back of the upstairs patio and all of the way to the back by the water.
2. If you miss the Country Bear Jamboree, remnants of the original show can be seen around the restaurant.

Harbour Galley
Description: Waterfront-style food with lobster entrées
Type: Fast service
Age Group: Everyone
Price: $
Recommendation: Lobster Bisque or Lobster Roll

Fantasyland

Theme: Magic makes memories in this classic kid-friendly land located behind the famous castle.

Rides

Matterhorn Bobsleds
Description: Swiss mountain-themed rollercoaster and Fantasyland's only thrill ride.
Level: Thrill (must be 42"/107cm or taller)
Recommendation: Board the left side (there are two tracks)
FastPass: Coming in 2017
★ **Magic Tip** ★
1. There are two separate tracks for the Matterhorn and they are slightly different.

2. The one track loads on the left (when you are looking at the mountain from the loading sides) is FASTER and WILDER.
3. The right side is a lot slower, so this may be good people who don't enjoy fast rides, but want to try it.

Peter Pan's Flight
Description: Fly along Peter Pan through London and Neverland on a pirate ship!
Level: Young Kids / Everyone
Recommendation: Perfect for all ages and a Disneyland classic that we even recommend to thrill-seekers.
FastPass: None
★ Magic Tip ★

Peter Pan's Flight can have one of the longest lines in the park. To avoid these, we recommend riding this first if you are with small children who may have short attention spans.

Dumbo the Flying Elephant
Description: Soar high while boarding Dumbo! Also hold a feather to help Dumbo take off.
Level: Young Kids / Everyone
Recommendation: Perfect for families with young children.
FastPass: None
★ Magic Tip ★
This attraction typically has very long lines and is a short ride. The only way to limit this is to get to Disneyland at the park's opening and ride Dumbo early.

Mad Tea Party (Tea Cups)
Description: Disneyland's famous tea cups inspired by Alice in Wonderland! Spin with your friends (up to 3-4 adults per tea cup).
Level: Kids / Everyone

Recommendation: Perfect for all ages and a Disneyland classic that we even recommend to thrill-seekers (the tea cups can spin *fast* or slow, depending on how hard you turn them).
FastPass: None
★ **Magic Tip** ★
1. Rumor has it that the FASTEST spinning one is the plain purple teacup (not the one with the flowers).

Alice in Wonderland
Description: Hop aboard the Caterpillar and see the whimsical story of Walt Disney's *Alice in Wonderland*.
Level: Kids / Everyone
Recommendation: perfect for all ages.
FastPass: None

Mr. Toad's Wild Ride
Description: Zip in a zany buggy that follows the story of Mr. Toad (from the 1949 animated film, *The Adventures of Ichabod and Mr. Toad*).
Level: Kids / Family
Recommendation: Perfect for all ages. It's a Disneyland-only classic ride (Disney World closed this attraction in 1998 and replaced it with the Many Adventures of Winnie the Pooh).
FastPass: None

Snow White's Scary Adventures
Description: Travel through the tale of *Snow White and the Seven Dwarfs*
Level: Kids / Family
Recommendation: Perfect for families with young children.
FastPass: None
★ **Magic Tip** ★
Look up at the window above the Snow White ride. You will see the Evil Queen pull the curtains back every few minutes.

Pinocchio's Daring Journey
Description: A slow-paced, but colorful ride that follows the story of Walt Disney's *Pinocchio*.
Level: Kids / Family
Recommendation: Perfect for families with young children.
FastPass: None

King Arthur Carrousel
Description: A classic carrousel with horses from *The Sword in the Stone*
Level: Kids / Family
Recommendation: Perfect for families with young children.
FastPass: None

Casey Jr. Circus Train
Description: Pretend you're a circus animal on this slow-paced train that takes you up and down the hills from the movie *Dumbo*.
Level: Kids / Family
Recommendation: Perfect for families with young children.
FastPass: None

Storybook Land Canal Boats
Description: A boat ride through Monstro the Whale's mouth views of miniature models of Disney's best movies.
Level: Kids / Family
Recommendation: Perfect for families with young children.
FastPass: None
Note: This ride closes during parades.

"it's a small world"
Description: A boat floats through several counties with children singing the "It's A Small World" theme song in different languages.
Level: Young Kids / Family

Recommendation: Perfect for families with young children. During the holiday season, this ride dazzles with lights and new costumes.
FastPass: None
★ **Magic Tips** ★
1. Some find this ride horribly annoying because of the endless singing children (we're not kidding!)
2. Look for characters like Ariel and Aladdin hidden throughout the ride.

Shows and Attractions

<u>**Sleeping Beauty Castle Walkthrough**</u>
Description: Walk through the Disneyland castle
Level: Family / Everyone
Recommendation: Walk through, see the art, and take a picture outside of the castle.
FastPass: None
★ **Magic Tips** ★
1. There is often a Disneyland photographer outside of the castle. He or she will take your picture for free (though you have to pay for the prints) and afterward, the cast member is happy to take a free photo of you with your camera or phone.

<u>**Fantasy Faire (with Royal Hall and Royal Theatre)**</u>
Description: The newest addition to Fantasyland with shows and treats. Meet Princesses in the Royal Hall and watch them perform lives shows (*Beauty and the Beast* and *Tangled*) in the Royal Theatre.
Level: Kids / Family
Recommendation: Perfect for children of all ages who love Disney Princess with bench seating.
FastPass: None

★ Magic Tips ★
1. Maurice's Treats Snack Cart serves some extremely delicious pastries!
2. Get a princess-themed Mickey Hat at the Fairy Tale Treasures Shop.

Bibbidi Bobbidi Boutique
Description: Dress up in princess clothing and makeup
Level: Kids and Young Kids
Recommendation: Perfect for children who are inspired Disney princesses (for pricing starting a $59.95, kids can get their makeup and hair done- and even a gown from their favorite Disney princess).
FastPass: None
★ Magic Tips ★
1. There are more packages, including a "Knight Package" and a "Frozen Package".
2. Make an appointment up to 60 days in advance by calling (714) 781-7895.

Pixie Hollow
Description: Meet Tinker Bell and her friends between high blades of grass.
Level: Kids and Young Kids
Recommendation: Great for kids the pixie fan of any age
FastPass: None

Fantasyland Theatre Presents: Mickey and the Magical Map
Description: A live action show starring Mickey Mouse and his friends.
Level: Family
Recommendation: Great for show lovers of all ages. Awesome special effects, singing, and dancing.
FastPass: None
Tip: Get there early for the best seating!

Restaurants and Eateries

Maurice's Treats
Description: European-style pastries served from a cart inspired by *Beauty and the Beast*.
Type: Fast service desserts
Age Group: Everyone
Price: $
Recommendation: Strawberry Twist and the Boysen Apple Freeze

Village Haus Restaurant
Description: Italian, German, and American-fusion restaurant
Type: Fast service
Age Group: Everyone
Price: $$
Recommendation: BLT Flatbread

Troubadour Tavern
Description: Italian, German, and American-fusion restaurant
Type: Fast service snacks
Age Group: Everyone
Price: $$
Recommendation: Bacon and Sour Cream Stuffed Baked Potato.

Mickey's Toontown

Theme: A cartoon town where guests can visit Mickey Mouse and his friends in their homes.

★ Magic Tips ★
1. Pull the lever near the fireworks and see what happens (sometimes you need to give it a few tugs).

2. Take a photo behind the jail cell bars.
3. Pry open crates, ring that door bell, and try to open the doors for big surprises!

Rides

Roger Rabbit's Car Toon Spin
Description: A "dark ride" where riders can spin the wheel and make the car turn on the track.
Level: Everyone
Recommendation: Great for kids and possibly some thrill-riders.
FastPass: Available

Gadget's Go Coaster
Description: A short, kid-friendly rollercoaster
Level: Kids and Young Kids (must be 35"/ 89cm or taller)
Recommendation: Great for kids, unless there is a long wait. This ride is very short and the line is often very long.
FastPass: None
★ **Magic Tip** ★ The seats on this coaster are tiny, so take caution when riding depending on your height/size.

Shows and Attractions

Mickey and Minnie's Houses
Description: Walk through their homes and meet them at the end for a picture!
Level: Family / Everyone
Recommendation: If you want to meet Mickey or Minnie Mouse, this is the best as they aren't often spotted around the parks in their classic clothes.
FastPass: None

Goofy's Playhouse, Donald's Boat, and Chip 'N Dale Treehouse
Description: Play areas with meet and greets with the characters
Level: Kids and Young Kids
Recommendation: great for kids to play and have fun.
FastPass: None
★ **Magic Tip** ★ Goofy is often found in his playhouse and typically will help your child slide down the slide if you ask (great photos!)

Restaurants and Eateries

Toontown Dining (food with kids in mind – even picky eaters):

Daisy's Diner ($) – The personal-sized pizzas are tasty

Pluto's Dog House ($) – Scrumptious hot dogs

Clarabelle's ($) – We recommend the Mickey Ice Cream Sandwich

For detailed information about these restaurants for kids, read the Family with Kids Guide (Chapter 13).

Tomorrowland

Theme: World of the Future that is perfect for thrill seekers and more. *Season of the Force* takes over with music and themes from *Star Wars*. Meet Storm Troopers and be part of unique attractions for a limited time.

Rides

Space Mountain
(The *Star Wars*-themed Hyperspace Mountain)
Description: A rollercoaster in the dark (Hyperspace Mountain has Star Wars special effects and music on the same rollercoaster track).
Level: Thrill Riders (must be 40"/ 102cm or taller)
Recommendation: See this attraction before Hyperspace Mountain becomes a theme of the past!
FastPass: Available
★ Magic Tip ★
  1. Get to the park early and grab a FastPass for Space Mountain. Thrill riders tend to like this ride the most and may want to ride it twice.

Star Tours – The Adventures Continue
Description: 3D Star Wars-themed motion simulation ride.
Level: Thrill Riders
Recommendation: Perfect for those who enjoy motion simulation rides.
FastPass: Available
Note: Each time you ride this attraction it's different. *Star Tours* has nine different planets and a new scene from *Star Wars: The Force Awakens* to experience.

Finding Nemo Submarine Voyage
Description: Nemo and friends join you underwater in this slow-paced ride filled with animation effects.
Level: Family
Recommendation: Great for all ages, but not for those who may be claustrophobic. Thrill riders may also want to skip this one for its slow pace.
FastPass: None

Autopia
Description: Where kids can drive cars around a track.
Level: Kids / Family (must be 32"/81cm or taller to ride) (must be 54"/137cm to drive alone)
Recommendation: Designed for kids to tweens, but with height restrictions.
FastPass: Yes

Buzz Lightyear Astro Blasters
Description: Compete against others in this fun Toy Story themed ride. It seems like it's for the kids, but it's fun for everyone to blast the laser guns and try to rack up the points.
Level: Everyone (including most thrill riders)
Recommendation: A crowd favorite with a generally short line.
FastPass: None

★ Magic Tips ★
1. Targets worth the most points are as follows:
    - Blue Diamond targets = 10,000 points
    - Purple Triangles targets = 5,000 points
    - Green Square targets = 1,000 points
    - Circle targets = 100 points
2. You can hit the targets as many times as you'd like (keep hitting the Blue Diamonds!)
3. Targets are worth more when they light up
4. Zurg is worth 50,000 points - if you can hit him! Toward the end of the ride, Emperor Zurg attacks and on his chest is a tiny target. Shoot that small spot and score big!

Astro Orbiter
Description: Orbit a solar system model on rocket ships (similar to Dumbo)
Level: Kids / Family
Recommendation: Fun for young children
FastPass: None

Shows and Attractions

Star Wars Launch Bay
Description: Take a photo with Chewbacca, Darth Vader, Boba Fett, or Kylo Ren (these characters may change throughout the year). Also see replicas of movie props and more.
Level: Family / Everyone
Recommendation: The best place to take a photo with a *Star Wars* character.
FastPass: None
Warning: Kylo Ren and Darth Vader may be too scary for very young children (yes, they are scary and in character!)

Tomorrowland Theater: Path of the Jedi
Description: A 10-minute film that ventures through the *Star Wars* franchise leading up to *The Force Awakens*.
Level: Everyone
Recommendation: A great place to cool down in air conditioning.
FastPass: None

Jedi Training Academy
Description: A stunning showdown between the Jedi and the Sith from *Star Wars*.
Level: Kids / Everyone
Recommendation: Your child could participate and dress as a Jedi to combat Darth Vader is a lightsaber!
FastPass: None
Note: Located at the stage by the Galactic Grill.

Restaurants and Eateries

Galactic Grill (*Star Wars* themed)
Description: American-style breakfast, lunch, and dinner
Type: Fast service
Age Group: Everyone (many kids' options)
Price: $$
Recommendation: Lars Family Breakfast Platter (Breakfast), First Order Specialty Burger (Lunch and Dinner)

Redd Rocket's Pizza Port
Description: Pizza, pasta, salads, and desserts
Type: Cafeteria Style
Age Group: Everyone (many kids' options)
Price: $$
Recommendation: Mega Pepperoni slice and a Side Salad
Note: The bread sticks look good, but they are fairly bland.

Chapter Ten
Disney California Adventure

Introduction

While Disneyland is the iconic theme park, Disney California Adventure is the new cool kid in town! The park opened in 2001 and now is home to 7 California and Pixar-themed lands (Buena Vista Street, Hollywood Land, "a bug's land", Cars Land, Paradise Pier, Pacific Wharf, and Grizzly Peak).

With even more Disney-themed rides that aren't found in any other park like the California Screamin' rollercoaster and Mickey's Fun Wheel, California Adventure brings sunny-themed surprises for everyone. Some say that Disney California Adventure is the "adult park" because of its edgier rides and delicious restaurants that serve beer, wine, and specialty cocktails. In fact, those 21 and older can take wine tours and order from full bars all inside of the park.

Thrill riders will love this side of the Disneyland Resort because of its rollercoaster with a loop, dangerous Tower of Terror, and the *Cars*-themed Radiator Springs Racers. However, there's something for everyone in Disney California Adventure from The Little Mermaid "dark ride" to high-flying Soarin'.

Buena Vista Street

Theme: the grand entrance inspired by 1920's Los Angeles when Walt Disney first arrived in California.

Rides:

Red Car Trolley
Thrill Level: Everyone
Recommendation: Kids might be fond of this trolley ride to Hollywood Land.
FastPass: None

Restaurants and Eateries

Carthay Circle Restaurant
Description: Disney California Adventure's signature dining location with some of the best entrees the Disneyland Resort has to offer.
Type: Table Service with adult beverages available
Age Group: Adults and Teens (kids' meals available)
Price: $$$$
Recommendations:
- Starter: Carthay Signature Fried Biscuits - flakey pastries with an unforgettable blend of bacon, white cheddar, and jalapeno. Served with sweet apricot honey butter.
- Entrée: all of the food here is delicious, but we recommend the Crispy Maple Leaf Duck Confit Salad for lunch or the Artichoke Crepes for dinner.
- Dessert: Warm Dulce de Leche Marshmallow Turnover.

★ Magic Tips ★
1. Carthay Circle has a fancy atmosphere, but no need to dress up. The Disneyland Resort expects to see the guests in their normal park attire.
2. We highly recommend booking a reservation before visiting the park at Disneyland.com (or call 714-781-DINE). You can book up to 60 days in advance.
3. If you can't get a reservation and the line is too long, Carthay Circle Lounge is a great al

Carthay Circle Lounge
Description: A snacks and bites lounge that many adults will enjoy. Serves sushi and alcohol drinks.
Type: Adult beverages and finger foods
Age Group: Adult
Price: $$$
Recommendation:
   Tostaditas with Mole Verde-braised Pork Cheeks –A Mexican entrée with queso and avocado.

Fiddler, Fifer, and Practical Café (serves Starbucks Coffee)
Description: Coffee shop
Type: Fast Service
Age Group: Everyone
Price: $
Recommendation: Spinach, Feta, and Cage-Free Egg White (breakfast wrap)

Fairfax Market
Description: A place to purchase healthy snacks and vegetarian options.
Type: "On-the-Go"
Age Group: Everyone
Price: $
Recommendation: Hummus to snack, coconut water to drink.

More Eateries:

Clarabelle's Hand Scooped Ice Cream ($) - We recommend the Oswald Sundae (also available in a souvenir holder shaped like a kitchen sink)

Mortimer's Fish Market ($) - A great place to pick up snacks and bottled water.

Hollywood Land

Theme: 1920's Hollywood with a back lot, theatre, and animation studio.

Rides:

Guardians of the Galaxy - Mission: Breakout
Coming Summer 2017
Description: Plummet 13 stories in this Marvel-themed thrill ride.
Level: Thrill riders (must be 40"/ 102cm or taller)
Recommendation: Only for those who love thrilling rides
FastPass: Available

Monsters, Inc. Mike & Sulley to the Rescue!
Description: Slow moving dark ride
Thrill Level: Kids / Family
Recommendation: Fun for kids and fans of the movie
FastPass: None

Shows and Attractions

Disney Animation
Description: A collection of animation-themed attractions
- **Animation Academy** - We highly recommend this attraction. A Disney animator shows you how to draw a character in a simple way. The best part is that you can keep your free animation paper! Or snap a photo of it and recycle the paper outside of the attraction.
- **Sorcerer's Workshop** - See how classic Disney animated movies were brought to film and even make a short animation of your own!
- ***Turtle Talk with Crush*** - Interact with Crush the turtle from *Finding Nemo* in this unique and hilarious theatre-like event designed for Young Kids.

Thrill Level: Everyone (Turtle Talk is more for young kids)
Recommendation: Classic Disney
FastPass: None
Note: Check outside the building for Animation Academy character drawing times.

Disney Junior - Live on Stage!
Description: A live action stage show designed for preschool aged children who love Disney Junior.
Thrill Level: Young Kids
Recommendation: Families with very young children only
FastPass: None

Frozen - Live at the Hyperion
Description: A live action stage show starring the characters of Frozen. Sing along with Anna, Elsa, and Olaf!
Thrill Level: Family
Recommendation: Any Frozen fan
FastPass: Yes

Restaurants and Eateries

Schmoozies
Description: Blended fruit drinks
Type: Fast Service snacks
Age Group: Everyone
Price: $
Recommendation: The Dynamic Duo - blend of pineapple and strawberries with low-fat yogurt.

Award Wieners
Description: Gourmet hot dogs and sausages
Type: Fast service
Age Group: Everyone
Price: $
Recommendations:
    Sicilian Sausage - Tastes like a delicious sausage pizza.

Studio Catering Co.
Description: Non-alcoholic drinks
Type: Fast Service snacks
Age Group: Everyone
Price: $
Recommendation: Wonderland Watermelon Frozen Lemonade - a delicious slushy that you can also get in an Alice in Wonderland souvenir cup.

Fairfax Market ($) - A place to purchase "On-the-Go" healthy snacks and vegetarian options.

"a bug's land"

Theme: Shrink down into the tall grass for a kid-friendly land themed after Pixar's *A Bug's Life*.

Rides

<u>Flik's Fun Fair</u>
Description: A kids play area with multiple rides:
Level: Young Kids / Family
Recommendation: for the young kids mainly (though many adults enjoy Heimlich's Chew Chew Train for the humor)

- **Heimlich's Chew Chew Train** - our most recommended ride in the zone. Hop aboard a caterpillar-shaped train while Heimlich hilariously guides you through his favorite food to eat. You can even smell the delicious treats!

- **Flik's Flyers** - Move up and down on hot air balloons.

- **Francis' Ladybug Boogie** – ladybug-shaped cars move riders in circles to music.

- **Princess Dot Puddle Park** - jump and splash in this wet zone (★ Magic Tip ★ this attraction is located next to the restrooms in case you need to dry off).

- **Tuck and Roll's Drive 'Em Buggies** - kid-friendly bumper cars.

Shows and Attractions

It's Tough to be a Bug!
Description: A 4D theatre show themed after Pixar's _A Bug's Life_.
Thrill Level: Everyone / Family
Recommendation: For those who love 3D movies
FastPass: None
Note: Often this theatre is changed to premier Disney film previews like with added 4D effects.

Restaurants and Eateries

Churro Cart: Also serves Coca-Cola® drinks

Cars Land

Theme: A beautiful land with a stunning Route 66 backdrop themed after Pixar's _Cars_.

Rides

Radiator Springs Racers
Description: High-Speed Simulated Race Car Ride
Level: Family / Thrill Riders (must be 40"/ 102cm or taller)
Recommendation: Cars Land might seem like it's for little kids, but this ride is for the thrill riders, too.
FastPass: Available
★ Magic Tips ★
　　1. The FastPass for the Radiator Springs Racers is _not_ near the ride. Travel to _It's Tough to be a Bug_ and get the pass there.

2. Get the FastPass at the beginning of the day. The Radiator Springs Racers passes typically run out *very* early (usually within the first hour of the park opening, even on less crowded days).
3. If you didn't get a FastPass, you may want to opt for the "Single Rider Line". You won't likely sit next to your friends/family (though rarely they will seat you together if 2 spots open), however, the line is much shorter than the regular line. Loading for Single Riders is at the start of the queue to the Radiator Springs Racers in Cars Land.
4. The racers seat up to 6 riders, 3 in each row (similar to Test Track at EPCOT in Walt Disney World).

Mater's Junkyard Jamboree
Description: Get flicked and whirled around while riding the back of Mater's truck.
Level: Kids / Family (must be 32"/ 81cm or taller)
Recommendation: Perfect for kids and thrill riders might also enjoy this unpredictable ride.
FastPass: None

Luigi's Rollickin Roaders
Description: Spin and move to the music in colorful cars. Each time is different!
Level: Kids / Family (must be 32"/ 81cm or taller)
Studio Catering Co. Perfect for kids.
FastPass: None

Restaurants and Eateries

Flo's V8 Café
Description: Classic American Diner
Type: Fast Service
Age Group: Everyone

Price: $$
Recommendations:
1. Breakfast – American Breakfast (bacon, eggs, potatoes, and a biscuit).
2. Lunch & Dinner – BBQ Pork Ribs (comes with Coca-Cola™ BBQ sauce and mashed potatoes).

Cozy Cone Motel
Description: Cone-shaped food booths that serve delicious snacks.
Type: Fast Service Snacks
Age Group: Everyone
Price: $
Recommendations: Churro (ask for the caramel sauce) and the Chili Cone Queso (beef or vegetarian chili with cheddar cheese and corn chips served in a bread bowl).

More Eateries:

Fillmore's Taste-In ($): Fast Service snacks, juice, and water.

Pacific Wharf

Theme: A San Francisco-style dock with restaurants and adult drinks.

★ Magic Tips ★
There is plenty of seating here though we recommend going outside of the lunch and dinner times to avoid the crowds (though this may not be an issue on less crowded day).
1. Lunch before 11.30am or after 2.30pm.
2. Dinner before 4.30pm or after 7:30pm.

3. Stop by the Ghirardelli® Soda Fountain and Chocolate Shop for a free sample piece of chocolate!

Shows and Attractions

The Bakery Tour
Description: Take a tour of the Boudin Bakery at Disney California Adventure.
Thrill Level: Everyone
Recommendation: Fun for bread-lovers
FastPass: None
★ **Magic Tip** ★ Get a free piece of sample bread on the tour!

Restaurants and Eateries

Alfresco Tasting Terrace
Description: Wines and bar snacks with a park view on the terrace
Type: Bar and Lounge
Age Group: Adults
Price: $$ - $$$$ (depending on the wine)
Recommendations:
1. Try a Disney Family Wine (21 and older)
2. Charcuterie Cheese Board (delectable prosciutto, chorizo, blue cheese, olives, walnuts, and more)

More Restaurants (Fast Service):

Cocina Cucamonga Mexican Grill ($$) - We recommend the Burrito Sonora with Beef (cheese and beef burritos served with refried beans and rice).

Lucky Fortune Cookery ($$) – Chinese food, we recommend an Asian Rice Bowl with chicken (similar to orange chicken served on steamed white rice).

Pacific Wharf Café ($$) – Made with the deliciously famous Boudin bread, we recommend the clam chowder or broccoli and cheese soup in a sourdough bread bowl.

Wine Country Trattoria ($$) – Try the Red Sangria (21 and older) and the Bolognese.

Adult Pours:

Pacific Wharf Distribution Co. ($) – Popular beer on tap for adults (21 and older).
Rita's Baja Blenders ($) – For a double shot of tequila, ask for the Grand Margarita (21 and older).
Sonoma Terrace ($) – Try a Local California Craft Beer (21 and older).
Mendocino Terrace ($$) – Wines (for 21 and older) and soft drinks. We recommend pairing wine with the Italian Meat and Cheese Box

Other Eateries:
Ghirardelli® Soda Fountain and Chocolate Shop ($) – Browse delicious chocolate gift or order a creamy soda. Also get a free chocolate sample when you enter!

Paradise Pier

Theme: the central land of Disney California Adventure with a boardwalk-style atmosphere.

Rides

California Screamin'
Description: A fast steel rollercoaster with big drops and a loop!
Level: Thrill Riders (must be 48"/ 122cm or taller)
Recommendation: The Disneyland Resort's only looped rollercoaster - a thrill rider's dream! Needless to say, it's not for those who don't enjoy intense rollercoasters.
FastPass: Available
★ **Magic Tip** ★
The "Single Rider Line" could save you time on a busy day. Look for the blue sign that says "Single Rider Line" on the left side of the queue (where the ride unloads passengers).

Toy Story Midway Mania!®
Description: A 4D game where riders attempt to score the most points by shooting at animated targets with a plunger canon.
Level: Everyone
Recommendation: All ages will enjoy this ride, including preschooler, families, and thrill riders. No recommended if you have trouble seeing with 3D glasses.
FastPass: Coming in 2017
★ **Magic Tips** ★ on how to score BIG:
   1. Many "pro" riders hold the plunger between two fingers with their palm facing them (be careful not to pull too hard of course!)
   2. Shoot the higher-point targets at the bottom of the screens.

3. Scene #1 (Hamm and Eggs) – Hitting the pigs on the fence will make a cat show that can be hit multiple times for big points.
4. Scene #2 (Rex and Trixie) – Pop the lava balloons on the volcano to make it erupt with 500-point balloons.
5. Scene #3 (Green Army Men) – Look for the yellow-tinted plates that are worth 2,000 points.
6. Scene #4 (Alien Ring Game) – On the far sides are rocket ships and aliens worth big points.
7. Scene #5 (Woody's Western Theme) – Aim for the doors of the saloon to reveal higher point targets. At the end of this scene there are mine carts that roll toward you. Look for the bats above the mine carts that are worth some major points.

Mickey's Fun Wheel

Description: A massive multi-colored Ferris wheel that has both swinging and stationary gondolas.
Level: Everyone
Recommendation: Thrill riders will love the swinging gondolas and slow-paced riders will enjoy the stationary ones.
FastPass: None

★ Magic Tips ★

1. The top makes for some amazing photos of the resort.
2. The line for this ride can be very long and slow paced. Unfortunately, because there is no FastPass or Single Rider Line, we've yet to discover a faster way to ride this attraction. It's recommended to ride at the start of the day after you get your FastPass for another attraction.
2. This ride may close in the early evening due to its use in the World of Color.
3. You can control the colors on the Fun Wheel at night by playing the "California Adventure Fun Wheel Challenge"

just before the World of Color show (see World of Color description for game details in this chapter).
4. If you get motion sickness easily, we don't recommend the swinging gondolas.

The Little Mermaid - Ariel's Undersea Adventure
Description: A family-friendly "dark ride" with bright colors, music, and the story of *The Little Mermaid*.
Level: Young Kids / Kids / Family
Recommendation: Great for families and fans of Disney's *The Little Mermaid*.
FastPass: None

Silly Symphony Swings
Description: Classic spinning carnival swings that fly around to orchestral music.
Level: Everyone (must be 40"/ 102cm or taller)
Recommendation: Everyone from kids to thrill riders will love this whirl of a ride.
FastPass: None
Note: Tandem swings available

King Triton's Carousel
Description: A classic carousel with sea life instead of horses.
Level: Kids / Family
Recommendation: Perfect for kids of all ages.
FastPass: None

Goofy's Sky School
Description: A twisting family-friendly rollercoaster.
Level: Kids / Thrill riders (must be 42"/ 1027m or taller)
Recommendation: perfect for Thrill riders of all ages
FastPass: Available
★ Magic Tips ★

1. Check the FastPass return time for Goofy's Sky School. Often, it's only an hour or so after the time you get the pass.
2. The seats can be a bit uncomfortable for larger riders.

Jumpin' Jellyfish
Description: Bob up and down on these jellyfish-shaped parachute seats.
Level: Young Kids / Kids
Recommendation: Perfect for kids of all ages
FastPass: None

Golden Zephyr
Description: Whirl in a giant, slow-paced circle on a metallic aircraft.
Level: Young Kids / Family
Recommendation: Perfect for young kids and those who enjoy slow rides.
FastPass: None

Shows and Attractions

World of Color
Description: A stunning nighttime water show that takes guests through several Disney films and dazzling technical effects!
Thrill Level: Everyone / Family
Recommendation: Must see for all
FastPass: Available. We recommend getting to the park at opening to guarantee a reserved spot as FastPass tickets run out quickly.
Get Preferred Viewing with **Dinner Packages** – Reserve a World of Color 3-course meal package to receive a voucher to the preferred viewing areas:

1. Book at Ariel's Grotto (our top recommendation), Carthay Circle Restaurant, or Wine Country Trattoria for the voucher.
2. Dessert Package ($79 per person) – choose from several different desserts and receive a sparkling beverage while you watch the show.

To book, visit Disneyland.com or call (714) 781-4565 up to 60 days in advance.

★ Magic Tips ★

To get the best view, start at Disney California Adventure when the park opens and reserve your FastPass. These often run out early, so make sure you reserve yours.

Note: Getting a FastPass to World of Color will *not* affect you getting any other passes throughout the day.

If you don't get reserved seating, there is only limited standing room, so make sure you get to your spot well ahead of time (we recommend at least 45 minutes before the start of the show).

Be Part of the Lighting Magic

- Get a "Made with Magic" Mickey or Minnie Mouse hat that light up with the show (Mickey Gloves light as well). These can be purchased at the park stores for $20-$30. They can also be purchased at the Main Street shops in Disneyland or Off the Page in Hollywood Land.

- Want to control the color? You can by playing a special online game with your mobile device. Connect to the "PierGames" Wi-Fi on your device (up to 45 minutes from show time) for the game to pop up in your browser. Use your memory skills to compete against others in the park. The winner will be able to control the colors of Mickey's Fun Wheel for 30 seconds!

Control the Colors on Mickey's Fun Wheel
A game that appears before the World of Color show begins.
1. 45 minutes before the start of the show, log your mobile device onto the Wi-Fi network, "PierGames".
2. Open your browser to play the game (no app download needed)
3. Play a color memory game against others in the park. The winner controls the colors of the Fun Wheel for 30 seconds!

Restaurants and Eateries

<u>Ariel's Grotto</u>
Description: American dining
Type: Table Service (Character dining also available for breakfast and lunch)
Age Group: Everyone (especially families with kids)
Price: $$$$
Recommendations:
- Breakfast – All-American Breakfast (hickory-smoked bacon or sausage, scrambled eggs, hash browns, and oats)
- Lunch – Red Oaked-Smoked Honey-Whisky Barbecue Tri-Tip (served with mashed potatoes and vegetables)
- Dinner – Grilled Lobster Tail and Red Oaked-Smoked Honey-Whisky Barbecue Tri Tip (served with mashed potatoes and vegetables)
- Cocktails – Magical Star Cocktail (passion fruit blend with coconut rum served over a glowing ice cube that you can keep) or Moscow Mule (vodka with ginger beer, lime, and agave nectar)

★ **Magic Tips** ★
1. Book in advance to avoid lines (Disneyland.com or call 714-781-DINE)

2. You can also get reserved seating for World of Color by booking your dinner reservation early.

Cove Bar
Description: Disney California Adventure's popular bar with a view of the water and Paradise Pier.
Type: Casual Table Service and Bar
Age Group: Adults and Teens (there are tasty non-alcoholic options for nondrinkers)
Price: $$
Recommendations:
1. CB Lobster Nachos - Zesty nachos supreme (tortilla chips, black beans, cheese blend, and chipotle crème) with many flavorful bits of lobster.
2. Trio of Tri-Tip Sliders - Made with bacon, arugula, and blue cheese.
3. Cocktails - Habanero Lime Margarita (Patron tequila, habanero lime, and sweet-and-sour) or Moscow Mule (vodka with ginger beer, lime, and agave nectar)
4. Non-Alcoholic Drink - Wild Strawberry Lemonade

★ **Magic Tip** ★ get to the bar before 11:30am to avoid the lines that begin around that time (even a short line can take an hour or more for seating).

Paradise Garden Grill
Description: A California-style grill.
Age Group: Everyone
Price: $$
Recommendations: Grilled Steak Skewer (served with rice, cucumber salad, and pita bread).

Corn Dog Castle
Description: get a delicious, battered hot dog with Disney's famous recipe.
Age Group: Everyone

Price: $
Recommendation: Corn Dog

Bayside Brews
Description: Popular beer on tap for adults (21 and older)
Age Group: Adult
Price: $
Recommendation: Many standard choices so we recommend picking your favorite brand.

Paradise Pier Ice Cream Company
Description: Come here your favorite flavor of soft-serve ice cream (or a root beer float).
Age Group: Everyone
Price: $
Recommendation: All of the ice cream is delicious so we'll leave it up to you and your mood in that moment!

Grizzly Peak

Theme: Californian national park-themed land. Get soaked on the Grizzly River Run or board the hang glider simulation, Soarin'!

★ **Magic Tip** ★ If you stay at the Grand Californian Hotel and Spa (or any other Disneyland Resort hotel), you can enter the park through an exclusive entrance that empties into Grizzly Peak via the Grand Californian Hotel.

Rides

Soarin'
Description: A hang glider simulation that takes you over stunning views, landmarks, and scents that fill the air.
Level: Everyone / Thrill Riders (must be 40"/ 102cm or taller)
Recommendation: A unique, must-see experience.
FastPass: Available
★ Magic Tip ★
1. Highly recommend getting a FastPass for this attraction as the line can get very long.
2. For the "Single Rider Line", ask a cast member at the FastPass entrance.

Grizzly River Run
Description: board a massive raft and travel up and down a gushing river.
Level: Everyone / Thrill Riders (must be 42"/ 107cm or taller)
Recommendation: Perfect for those who love water rides.
FastPass: Available
★ Magic Tip ★
1. The Single Rider Line is available by walking up the stairs to the exit of the ride just before the rotating platform.
2. On colder days, a FastPass is often not needed as this ride typically doesn't have a very long lines in cooler weather.

Redwood Creek Challenge Trail
Description: Inspired by the Pixar movie, *Up* and Disney's *Brother Bear*, kids can earn Wilderness Explorer badges by completing challenges.
Level: Kids / Family
Recommendation: A playground for kids of all ages.
FastPass: None

Restaurants and Eateries

Smokejumpers Grill
Description: A hanger-shaped American grill for burgers, fries, and more
Type: Fast Service
Age Group: Everyone
Price: $$
Recommendations: Bacon Cheddar Burger and Chili-Cheese Fries

Refreshment Point ($) – Coca Cola beverages

Chapter Eleven
Downtown Disney

Introduction to Downtown Disney

Downtown Disney is the premier hangout location at the Disneyland Resort. It's surrounded by the resort hotels, bursting with shops including World of Disney, and filled with treats like an enormous Starbucks and tasty Jamba Juice. Also catch live entertainment at the House of Blues®, watch a movie at the AMC Theatre, or play arcade games and watch live sports games at the ESPN Zone. Best of all, theme park admission isn't required to visit Downtown Disney.

Dress Code: No need to dress up! Come in your Disneyland-approved theme park clothing.

Restaurants

Catal Restaurant – *Top Choice!*
Description: American and Mediterranean entrées
Type: Table Service
Age Group: Everyone
Price: $$$
Adult Beverages: Yes
Reservations: Disneyland.com or (714) 781-3463
Recommendations:
> Starter: Crispy Calamari
> Entrée: Crispy Suckling Pig (pork and roasted Brussel sprouts) or the Marinated Angus Hangar Steak (served with mashed potatoes)

Earl of Sandwich® – *Top Choice!*
Description: American Sandwiches
Type: Fast Service
Age Group: Everyone
Price: $
Adult Beverages: Yes (Beer and Wine)
Recommendation: The Earl Club (turkey, bacon, Swiss cheese hot sandwich)

ESPN Zone
Description: American sports-themed restaurant and bar. The upstairs section has sports-themed arcade games.
Type: Table Service / Lounge
Age Group: Everyone
Price: $$ - $$$
Adult Beverages: Yes (full bar with beer on tap)
Recommendation: Smokehouse Burger (savory bacon, cheddar, and barbecue sauce burger service with fries or a salad)

Rainforest Café
Description: Dine in a rainforest filled with lush plants, waterfalls, and animatronics that come to life when the occasional storms brews in the restaurant! Perfect for families with kids though fine-diners may want to skip this one.
Type: Table Service
Age Group: Family (kids will especially love this place)
Price: $$
Adult Beverages: Yes (Wine and Beer)
Reservations: Disneyland.com or (714) 772-0413
Recommendation: Get a seat next to the aquarium.

La Brea Bakery Café
Description: Brunch and dinner menus
Type: Casual Service
Age Group: Everyone
Price: $$
Adult Beverages: Yes
Recommendation: Margherita Pizza
Note: Get Fast Service sandwiches at the La Brea Bakery Express next door.

Naples Ristorante e Pizzeria
Description: Italian
Type: Table Service
Age Group: Everyone
Price: $$$
Adult Beverages: Yes
Recommendation: get your favorite type of pizza

Napolini
Description: Pizzas
Age Group: Everyone
Type: Table Service
Price: $$

Adult Beverages: No
Recommendation: get your favorite type of pizza

Ralph Brennan's Jazz Kitchen®
Description: Cajun food with a lounge bar
Type: Table Service / Lounge
Age Group: Adults and teenagers (though they have options for kids)
Price: $$
Adult Beverages: Yes
Reservations: Disneyland.com or (714) 781-3463
Recommendation: Fried Chicken Po-Boy or Creole Chicken Caesar Wrap
Note: For fast service sandwiches, visit the Jazz Kitchen Express next door.

Tortilla Jo's
Description: Mexican food with a lounge bar
Type: Table Service / Lounge
Age Group: Everyone
Price: $$
Adult Beverages: Yes
Reservations: Disneyland.com or (714) 781-3463
Recommendation:
- Fajita de Tres (sizzling chicken, steak, and shrimp served with corns tortillas, rice, and beans)
- Shredded Beef Burrito (served with rice and refried beans) or the TJ's Grilled Chicken Caesar Salad

Note: For Fast service Mexican food, visit the Taqueria next door.

Crossroads at House of Blues®
Description: Cajun and American
Type: Table Service
Age Group: Adults and Teenagers
Price: $$$

Adult Beverages: Yes
Recommendations:
    Starter: Three Angus Sliders
    Entrée: Buttermilk Fried Chicken

Drinks and Other Eateries

Starbucks® ($) – Coffee, pastries, and breakfast sandwiches

Jamba Juice ($) – Blended fruit smoothies

Haagen-Dazs® ($) – Ice cream

Uva Bar ($$) – A cool outdoor bar with breakfast, lunch, and dinner options.

The Voodoo Lounge at the House of Blues® ($) – A full New Orleans-themed lounge bar

Wetzel's Pretzels ($) – Savory and sweet pretzels

Shops

<u>Disney Shops:</u>

World of Disney® – This ultimate Disney store is massive and located close to the parks
Anna & Elsa's Boutique – Disney collectables and apparel
Disney Vault 28 – Unique Disney collectables
Disney's Pin Traders – A place to buy Disney pins
D-Street – Hip Disney apparel and collectables

Fun Shops:

Build-A-Bear Workshop® – Design your own plush teddy bear
The LEGO® Store – Purchase and play with building blocks. Also check out the enormous Disney characters made entirely of Legos!
RIDEMAKERZ® – Customize your own toy car
WonderGround Gallery – Disney Art for viewing and for sale.
Marceline's Confectionery – Pick through a wide assortment of candy and gifts.

Mall Shops:

Quiksilver® – Beach-inspired apparel and swimsuits
Fossil® – Leather apparel and accessories
Sanuk® – Shoes and sandals
Something Silver® – Jewelry and accessories
Sunglass Icon® – Sunglasses and accessories
Sephora® – Makeup and beauty supplies
Rainforest Café® Retail Shopping Village – Collectables and apparel

More Fun:

AMC Theatre 12 – Grab some popcorn and see a movie located near the Disneyland Hotel. www.amctheatres.com
Stages – During the day and at night, Downtown Disney comes alive with live music
House of Blues® – See a live concert or attend an event. List of shows: www.houseofblues.com/anaheim

Hotel Restaurants – Visit one of the 3 resort hotels and dine at one of their restaurants, stop at a bar, or recline in a lounge.

Chapter Twelve
Disney Character Locations

Introduction

You can meet most of your favorite Disney characters at the resort. They are always happy to sign autographs, interact, and take a photo with you. Disneyland is home to all of the classics from Mickey and Minnie to Donald and Daisy. But it doesn't stop there! Princesses roam Fantasyland while Stormtroopers from *Star Wars* stomp the Tomorrowland grounds. In Disney California Adventure's Hollywood Land, you can even meet Marvel's Spiderman and Captain America. Aren't sure if you should meet a character? We recommend it! After greeting Mickey, Chewbacca, or a Disney Princess, even an adult will have a smile that won't go away!

Magic Tips for Easily Finding Characters

1. Download the Disneyland App on your mobile device to track the characters!

2. Many of them have "show times" in certain locations. Be sure to check the character times on your resort map before visiting.
3. Character dining in the Disneyland Hotels and in the theme parks have many characters who will interact with you while you eat.
4. You may also see them walking around the parks or in the shows and parades.
5. Sadly, not every character comes out each day. However, one of your favorites is sure to be there!

Character Locations (alphabetical)

Aladdin - Aladdin's Oasis (Adventureland)
Anna - Animation Academy (Disney California Adventure)
Ariel - Ariel's Grotto (Disney California Adventure)
Baloo - Adventureland (Disneyland)
Belle - Princess Fantasy Faire (Disneyland)
Boba Fett - Star Wars Launch Bay (Disneyland)
Buzz Lightyear - Tomorrowland (Disneyland)
Captain America - Hollywood Land (Disney California Adventure)
Chewbacca - Star Wars Launch Bay (Disneyland)
Chip 'n Dale - Chip 'n Dale Critter Breakfast at Storyteller's Café (Disney's Grand Californian Hotel)
Cruella de Ville - Hollywood Land (Disney California Adventure)
Crush the Turtle - *Turtle Talk with Crush* at Disney Animation (Disney Hollywood Studios)
Daisy Duck - Toon Town (Disneyland)
Donald Duck - Donald's Boat in Toon Town (Disneyland)
Duffy the Bear - Paradise Pier (Disneyland)
Darth Vader - Jedi Training / Star Wars Launch Bay (Disneyland)
Eeyore - Critter Country (Disneyland)

Elsa – Animation Academy (Disney California Adventure)
Elastigirl (Pixar's *The Incredibles*) – Hollywood Land (Disney California Adventure)
Flik (Pixar's *A Bug's Life*) – "a bug's land" (Disney California Adventure)
Frollo (*The Hunchback of Notre Dame*) – Halloween Time (Disneyland, mid-September - October 31st)
Frozone (The Incredibles) – Hollywood land (Disney California Adventure)
Goofy – Goofy's Playhouse in Toon Town (Disneyland)
Handy Manny – Hollywood Land (Disney California Adventure)
Jack Sparrow – New Orleans Square (Disneyland)
Jack Skellington – Holiday time in front of the Haunted Mansion (Disneyland, September - December)
Kylo Ren – Star Wars Launch Bay (Disneyland)
Princess Jasmine – Aladdin's Oasis (Disneyland)
Lightning McQueen – see him driving around Cars Land (Disney California Adventure)
Mad Hatter – Fantasyland (Disneyland)
Mary Poppins – Fantasyland (Disneyland)
Mater – Cars Land (Disney California Adventure)
Meeko (*Pocahontas*) – Character Breakfast at the Storyteller's Café (Disney's Grand Californian Hotel)
Mickey Mouse – at his home in Toon Town (Disneyland)
Minnie Mouse – at her home in Toon Town (Disneyland)
Mr. Potato Head – interact with him in the queue for Toy Story Midway Mania™ (Disney California Adventure)
Oswald the Lucky Rabbit – Buena Vista Street (Disney California Adventure)
Peter Pan – Fantasyland (Disneyland)
Piglet – Critter Country (Disneyland)
Pluto – Toon Town (Disneyland)
Prince Phillip – Fantasyland (Disneyland)
Prince Naveen – New Orleans Square (Disneyland)

Queen of Hearts – Fantasyland (Disneyland) and Hollywood Land (Disney California Adventure)
Sally (The Nightmare Before Christmas) – Holiday time in front of the Haunted Mansion (Disneyland, September – December)
Sleeping Beauty – Princess Fantasy Faire (Disneyland)
Snow White – Main Street, U.S.A. or Princess Fantasy Faire (Disneyland)
Spider-man – Hollywood Land (Disney California Adventure)
Stormtroopers – Tomorrowland (Disneyland)
Sulley – Hollywood Land (Disney California Adventure)
Tiana – New Orleans Square (Disneyland)
Tigger – Critter Country (Disneyland)
Tinker Bell and her friends – Pixie Hallow (Disneyland)
Winnie the Pooh – Critter Country (Disneyland)

More Magic Tips

- Kids will love the character autograph books sold on Main Street.
- During the holidays, characters are often dressed in seasonal outfits (Halloween, Christmas, and other special days).
- The Princess Fantasy Faire is the best way to take a photo with a Disney Princess.
- If you love villains, come during Halloween (mid-September through October 31st) to see more of them roaming the parks.
- Star Wars characters tend to stick to Tomorrowland in Disneyland. Chewbacca loves to give hugs but Darth Vader and Kylo Ren are quite intimidating!
- Marvel characters (like Spider-man and Captain America) often change. For instance, Thor makes appearances and Disney may introduce other Marvel characters to replace previous ones.

Chapter Thirteen
Family with Kids Guide

Introduction

The Disneyland Resort is known for being the "The Happiest Place on Earth" and we truly believe that it is! Part of Walt Disney's vision was to provide a place for families to enjoy themselves with fun for everyone. Many of the rides at Disneyland are designed for the kid in us all, but this section is all about children from babies to ten-year-olds. Using this guide can help you have a pleasant stay with your children.

Note: This section has brief ride descriptions aimed for the age group. For more descriptions, as well as Magic Tips on attractions and restaurant recommendations, see the full details on the resort pages.

Babies and Toddlers

We hear a lot of parents ask: "Should I bring my baby to Disneyland?" Many parents love bringing their babies to the parks! If you decide to bring your baby to the resort, here is a list of what to bring, do, and all about the baby care centers.

What to Bring:

Protection from the Sun – We recommend sunscreen, hats, blankets, and a covered stroller to keep your little one comfortable.

Blankets and Warm Clothes – These items are essential for cooler days (or at night when the temperatures drop).

Diapers, Wipes, and a Change of Clothes – Just in case of a mess, a change of clothes can be a lifesaver.

Bottles and Formula – Don't forget the liners!

Baby Food – The Disneyland Resort will allow small glass jars as long as they contain baby food.

Backpack – This is for you to carry your baby's items. Sometimes you can hide these in a stroller, but just in case you leave your stroller for a ride, we recommend carrying your items with you.

Stroller – Rentals start at $15 a day or bring your own. Fantasyland has several locations for parking your stroller while you wait in line. Cast members patrol the area for safety.

The Disneyland Baby Care Center

Just in case you forget something, Disneyland is equipped with nannies that are there to help. Get baby food, diapers, wipes, and even medicine in these spots. They offer nursing rooms, changing tables, highchairs for feeding, a microwave, water, and more.

Locations:

Disneyland – Main Street, U.S.A., next to First Aid.

Disney California Adventure – In the Pacific Wharf, next to the Ghirardelli Store.

Changing Rooms – These are found in most restrooms (men and women).

Breast Feeding – Feeding your baby is a top priority and you shouldn't be nervous to do so at Disneyland. If you want privacy (or quiet), head to the Baby Care Centers in the parks.

First Aid – Located next to the Baby Care Center in Disneyland on Main Street, U.S.A.

Emergencies – If you experience an emergency, call 911.

Rides for Babies and Toddlers

<u>"it's a small world"</u> (Fantasyland) – A gentle boat ride with colors and singing children.

<u>The Many Adventures of Winnie the Pooh</u> (Critter Country) – A slow ride through the story of Winnie the Pooh. See his friends from Tigger to Piglet in this cute and florescent ride.

<u>Dumbo the Flying Elephant</u> (Fantasyland) – Circle round while flying on Dumbo. This ride was designed for kids, but the line can be long.

Mickey's Toontown – Meet Mickey, Minnie, Donald, and Goofy in this toddler-friendly zone. Also a great place for kid-friendly meals.

"a bug's land" (Disney California Adventure) – Several gentle rides and a splash area perfectly designed for young kids. We recommend Heimlich's Chew Chew Train (even adults love this one for the humor and delicious smells).

Carousels: King Triton's Carousel (Disney California Adventure) and King Arthur's Carousel (Disneyland) are two classic carousels, one in each park.

Jungle Cruise (Adventureland) – A slow moving boat through the African and Amazonian wilds.

Pirates of the Caribbean – A long, dark ride on a boat with two drops at the beginning. If you think these will startle your baby, it's best to avoid it.

Disneyland Railroad – An easy ride around the perimeter of Disneyland (closed for refurbishment in until Summer 2017).

More Tips for Babies and Toddlers

See a Show or Parade – With wonderful music and dancing characters, your baby or toddler will be delighted. Disney Junior: Live on Stage (Disney California Adventure) is a live stage show designed for toddlers. Check the map for a schedule of shows and parades.

Don't Try to Do It All – Young kids can love Disneyland, but that doesn't mean they'll have the energy for a continuous, all-day outing. Space out rides and times waiting in line for simple joys like looking at the baby ducks in the moat around Sleeping Beauty's Castle or eat a snack under some shade.

Take a Break – As a parent you know that babies and toddlers can wear out fast. At the Disneyland Resort, this is no exception. Plan to go back to the hotel, hang under the shade of trees or umbrellas, or find the Baby Care Center for some peace and quiet. When your baby is ready to go again, head back to the park until he or she is spent.

Rider Switch

Do you have a young child with you, but all of the adults in your party want to ride? Many Disneyland Resort rides give you the option to wait and switch places when finished. Here is a list:

Disneyland:
- Autopia
- Big Thunder Mountain Railroad
- Gadget's Go Coaster
- Indiana Jones Adventure
- Matterhorn Bobsleds
- Space Mountain
- Splash Mountain
- Star Tour – The Adventures Continue

Disney California Adventure
- California Screamin'
- Goofy's Sky School
- Grizzly River Run
- Luigi's Rollickin' Roadsters
- Jumpin' Jellyfish
- Mater's Junkyard Jamboree
- Radiator Springs Racers
- Silly Symphony Swings
- Soarin'
- Tuck and Roll's Drive 'Em Buggies

Kids (Ages 3-9)

Since every kid is different, their interests with Disneyland may vary greatly. Many children love fast rides while others look forward to meeting their favorite characters. With so much to do at the Disneyland Resort, we've narrowed it down to the best ideas.

In this section you will note the numbers next to the rides and attractions. We've numbered the rides in order of how kid-friendly they are. #1 will be the most kid friendly, and the higher numbers are less kid-friendly. The descriptions are there to help you make the best judgment for your child.

Disneyland with Kids Guide

Main Street, U.S.A.
This land is filled with souvenir shops and places to eat.

1. The Magic Shop – for fun games!
2. Horse-drawn street cars – for leisurely strolls

    Visit the Gibson Girl Ice Cream Parlor for sweets.

    Carnation Café is great for burgers, fries, and salads.

    Plaza Inn – has character breakfasts with "Minnie and Friends" (book this early on Disneyland.com).

Fantasyland
This land has rides for all ages, but especially geared for kids.

1. Fantasy Faire – Meet your favorite Disney Princesses.

2. Peter Pan's Flight, Pinocchio's Daring Journey, Snow White's Scary Adventures, Alice in Wonderland, and Mr. Toad's Wild Ride are all family-friendly "dark rides".
3. Storybook Land Canal Boats – A slow-moving guided boat ride around miniature sets from Disney movies.
4. Casey Jr. Circus Train – A slow-moving train ride through a green hillside and back.
5. Dumbo the Flying Elephant – Fly around and around while holding Dumbo's flying feather on this classic attraction.
6. Pixie Hollow – Meet Tinker Bell and her pixie friends.
7. Mad Tea Party – The classic Disneyland tea cups. You can control how fast you spin the tea cup by turning the wheel in the center.
8. The Matterhorn Bobsleds – If your child enjoys slower rollercoasters, the right side of the Matterhorn is less intense than the left. However, this ride does feature a scary Abominable Snowman (must be 42" / 107cm or taller).

★ Magic Tip ★

We don't recommend eating in Fantasyland with your kids because it is so stimulating. The carts are fine for popcorn, churros, drinks, and other snacks, but the Village Haus is so close to rides and the castle that it may be difficult to get them to settle down and eat. Choose Mickey's Toontown instead.

Critter Country

A small, mostly kid-friendly land.

1. The Many Adventures of Winnie the Pooh – Perfect for kids who love slow, colorful rides with happy critters.
2. Splash Mountain – You will get wet on this log ride with many drops and a massive one at the end! The theme is generally colorful and happy throughout (must be 40"/102cm or taller).

Hungry Bear Restaurant – A great place for families to eat. Plenty of picnic tables and a great selection of burgers, wraps, and entrees designed for kids.

Mickey's Toontown

Another great area with characters, rides, and food designed for kids.

1. Take a picture with Mickey and Minnie Mouse in their interactive homes.
2. Visit play areas for kids including Donald's Boat, Goofy's Playground, and Chip N' Dale Treehouse.
3. Toontown is filled with kid-friendly eateries and tables for eating.
4. Roger Rabbit's Car Toon Spin – a family-friendly "dark ride" with a wheel to spin the car.
5. Gadget's Go Coaster – a short, family-friendly rollercoaster with a typically long line (must be 35"/89cm to ride).

★ **Magic Tip** ★

Toontown is home to hot dogs, pizza, and kids' meals that are specially designed for each hungry child. See page 135.

Adventureland

A jungle-themed area with a couple of great attractions with kids and families in mind.

1. Tarzan's Treehouse™ – loved by kids who enjoy climbing.
2. Jungle Cruse – A riverboat ride designed for all ages.
3. Indiana Jones™ Adventure is perfect for kids who love thrill rides (must be 46"/117cm or taller).

Bengal Barbecue – Offers tasty snacks from breadsticks, pretzels, and skewers kids will love.

New Orleans Square
This land is filled with great places to eat for those who enjoy creole and French dining.

1. Pirates of the Caribbean – a music-filled pirate-themed boat ride with two drops at the beginning. Has many dark spots, but is generally not scary.
2. Haunted Mansion – a slow-moving ride through a haunted mansion that may frighten young kids.

    Café Orleans – Several choices for kids from macaroni and cheese to chicken breasts.

Frontierland
Jump into the wild west in this land filled with runaway trains, cowboys, and plenty of space for families to eat!

1. Pirate's Lair on Tom Sawyer's Island (under renovation until Summer 2017) – An island playground with bridges and hiding spots designed for kids of all ages. You must take a raft to the island and back.
2. Big Thunder Mountain – A fast-moving rollercoaster labeled "the wildest ride in the wilderness". This is a family-friendly rollercoaster with no loops or big drops (must be 40"/102cm or taller).
3. The Golden Horseshoe is a perfect restaurant with plenty of seating for the whole family as well as options for kids' meals (Chicken Nuggets or the Power Pack).

Tomorrowland

While this land is known for its thrills, Tomorrowland offers a variety of rides and attractions for the entire family.

1. Finding Nemo Submarine Voyage – A family-friendly slow-moving ride in a submarine starring Nemo and his friends. Not recommended for those who don't enjoy enclosed spaces.
2. Jedi Training Academy – A live show where kids (ages 4 – 12) can volunteer to become Jedis and battle Darth Vader. Look on the map for show times and you can eat at the Galactic Grill while watching the show.
3. Star Wars Launch Bay – meet and take a photo with Chewbacca or Kylo Ren, see prop replicas from *The Force Awakens*, and shop *Star Wars* collectables.
4. Astro Orbiter – A spinning rocket ride similar to Dumbo the Flying Elephant.
5. Buzz Lightyear Astro Blasters – A slow-moving family-friendly "dark ride" where riders shoot a laser gun at targets to rack up points.
6. Autopia – A ride where kids can drive cars around a track (must be 32"/81cm to drive and 54"/137cm or taller to drive alone).
7. *Star Tours*: The Adventures Continue – A 3D motion simulation ride through two scenes inspired by *Star Wars*. Contains loud noises and lighting effects (must be 40"/102cm or taller to ride).
8. Space Mountain – A fast-moving rollercoaster in the dark. This classic ride is now *Star Wars*-themed as "Hyperspace Mountain" with added special effects and music from the movies (must be 40"/102cm or taller to ride).

Redd Rockett's Pizza Port – Cafeteria Style pizza, salads, pasta, sweets, and drinks with plenty of indoor and outdoor seating.

Galactic Grill – Hamburgers, fries, and meals for kids served hot at this fast service restaurant with plenty of tables and seats.

California Adventure Guide with Kids

Buena Vista Street
This land is filled with souvenir shops and places to eat.

1. Red Car Trolley – A slow ride to Hollywood Land that young children may enjoy.
2. The Pixar Play Parade – Watch your favorite Pixar characters in this upbeat dance and music parade. Check the map for show times.
3. Visit Clarabelle's Hand-Scooped Ice Cream for sweets.

"a bug's land"
A kid-friendly land stylized from Pixar's *A Bug's Life*.

1. *It's Tough to be a Bug!* – A hilarious 3D theatre show designed for the whole family.
2. Flik's Fun Fair – A collection of rides designed for kids of all ages. However, young thrill riders may not enjoy this land.
   - Heimlich's Chew Chew Train – A funny ride on a caterpillar through his favorite scented foods.
   - Francis' Ladybug Boogie – Spinning ladybug cars.
   - Princess Dot Puddle Park – Perfect for kids who love to get wet! Luckily, it's located next to a bathroom for easy drying.
   - Flik's Flyers – Move around in a circles in the sky on simulated hot air balloons.
   - Tuck and Roll's Drive 'Em Buggies – Kid-sized bumper cars.

Paradise Pier

The largest land of Disney California Adventure, based around a waterfront and home of definitive rides and the spectacular World of Color night show.

1. World of Color – A stunning nighttime water show filled with Disney characters and color that's a perfect fit for the entire family.
2. The Little Mermaid: Ariel's Undersea Adventure – A family-friendly slow-moving "dark ride" through the story and music of Disney's *The Little Mermaid*.
3. King Triton's Carousel – A classic carousel with fish instead of horses.
4. Golden Zephyr – A slow-moving ship that spins in circles on a cable. This is family-friendly and perfect for toddlers, however, could be boring for kids who enjoy thrill rides.
5. Mickey's Fun Wheel – A Ferris wheel with two different experiences. For kids who love thrill rides, choose a swinging gondola. For kids that don't like fast movement, choose a stationary gondola. Not recommended for children who do not enjoy heights.
6. Toy Story Midway Mania!® – A 4D target practice based on Pixar's *Toy Story*. Kids of all ages will enjoy this ride, though not recommended for those that have trouble seeing with 3D glasses.
7. Jumpin' Jellyfish – Older children will enjoy these dropping jellyfish. Not recommended for those who don't enjoy heights (must be 40"/102cm or taller).
8. Silly Symphony Swings – Spin around over land and water on these orchestrated swings. Not recommended for children who do not enjoy heights (must be 40"/102cm).
9. Goofy's Sky School – A kid-friendly rollercoaster with sharp turns and small dips (must be 42"/107cm or taller).
10. California Screamin' – A high-speed rollercoaster with larger dips and a loop (must be 48"/122cm to ride).

Boardwalk Pizza and Pasta – Serves up hot pizzas, salads, and kid-sized meatball sandwiches.

Pacific Wharf

A land reminiscent of San Francisco wharfs. This area is filled with food mainly aimed at adults, however most have great options for kids.

Cocina Cucamonga Mexican Grill
Toddler Meal – Chicken and Rice
Kids' Meals – Bean Cheese Burrito or Chicken Quesadilla

Lucky Fortune Cookery
Style: Asian
Kids' Meal – Chicken and Brown Rice

Pacific Wharf Distribution Co.
Toddler Meal – Cheesy Macaroni
Kids' Meal – Turkey sandwich or "power pack" with smoothie, apples, carrots, banana, and crackers.

Cars Land

Set to the beautiful, mountainous landscape of Route 66, Cars Land is as breathtaking as it is fun for the entire family.

Note: Pay attention to the height restrictions, as each ride in Cars Land has them.

1. Mater's Junkyard Jamboree – Flick and turn on this unpredictable ride. Perfect for kids who enjoy fast-moving rides (must be 32"/81cm or taller to ride).
2. Luigi's Rollickin' Roadsters – A new attraction where cars dance and turn to the music. Perfect for kids (must be 32"/81cm or taller to ride).

3. Radiator Springs Racers – Race along the stars of Pixar's *Cars* in this "dark ride" and thrill ride combination that the entire family will love. It is not recommended for those who don't enjoy fast-moving rides (must be 40"/102cm or taller).

Cozy Cone Motel – Pick up snacks in orange traffic cones from churros, drinks, soft-serve ice cream, queso, pretzel bites, frozen drinks, and popcorn.

Fillmore's Taste-In – A fruit and beverage cart.

Flo's V8 Café – A diner with plenty of indoor and outdoor seating
Kids' Meals:
Breakfast – Scrambled Eggs, Turkey Bacon, Potatoes, and fruit or a fruit plate with yogurt and a bran muffin.
Lunch/Dinner – Roast Beef Sandwich, Turkey Sandwich, or Macaroni and Cheese.

Hollywood Land

From glamour, film studios, and decrepit buildings, this land captures the true spirit of Hollywood.

1. Monsters, Inc. Mike and Sulley to the Rescue! – A "dark ride" with vibrant colors following the story of Pixar's *Monsters, Inc*. Kids of all ages will enjoy this ride, though young thrill riders may want to skip it.
2. Disney Animation Building:
    a. *Turtle Talk with Crush* – A hilarious interactive show designed for kids 3-9.
    b. Sorcerer's Workshop – Make your own animation and record your voice over a Disney film.
    c. Animation Academy – Learn to draw a Disney character from a live Disney Cartoonist. Older kids may find more enjoyment from this classroom environment.

Award Wieners – Hot dogs and more
> <u>Kids Meals</u> – Turkey Dog or a "power pack" with a smoothie, apples, carrots, banana, and crackers.

Schmoozies – Delicious fruit smoothies.

Fairfax Market – A fruit and beverage stand.

Grizzly Peak

Venture into California's wilderness, complete with redwoods and roaring rapids, all surrounding a bear-shaped mountain.

1. Redwood Challenge Trail – Kids can climb, play, and earn badges by completing tasks. Perfect for kids of all ages.
2. Soarin' – A hang glider simulation for the entire family. Not recommended for those who don't enjoy heights or brief periods of darkness (must be 40"/102cm or taller).
3. Grizzly River Run – A raft-based rapids adventure ending in a giant splash. Not recommended for those who don't enjoy getting wet or big drops (must be 40"/102cm or taller to ride)

Smokejumpers Grill – American hamburgers and more
<u>Kids' Meals</u> – Chicken Nuggets, Kid's Hamburger, or a "power pack" with a smoothie, apples, carrots, banana, and crackers.

Chapter Fourteen
Adult Guide to the Disneyland Resort

Introduction

The Disneyland Resort may be family-friendly but that doesn't mean it isn't also an adult retreat. From dive bars to thrill rides to fine-dining, the Disneyland Resort has what you're looking for! In this section we outline adult activities from the best places to drink to avoiding families with children.

Note: The Disneyland Park does not serve alcohol, however, Disney California Adventure and Downtown Disney have many options for wine, beer, and cocktails (must be 21 years of age or older with a valid ID to drink).

Parents' Evening Out

If you're an adult with children, part of your perfect Disneyland Resort vacation might be a night without them. If you're interested in heading back to the parks, Disneyland and Disney California

Adventure are often open until midnight. Or, perhaps you'd settle for a dinner alone with your significant other.

Whatever you choose to do with your time, there are great options for kids without their parents inside the resort. We recommend planning the night ahead of time to ensure you can have an easy transition into your night alone.

Pinocchio's Workshop
A place just for kids – without the parents!
Location: Disney's Grand Californian Hotel and Spa
- Kids make arts and crafts while parents can enjoy an evening at the Resort.
- Open from 2pm - 11pm, kids ages 5-12 are invited to participate.
- $15/hour per child (children must be potty-trained, feed himself or herself, and respectful to others).
- Plan a reservation in advance by calling (714) 635-2300 or make a reservation with Guest Services.

Babysitters
Disneyland does not have a babysitting service (outside of Pinocchio's Workshop), however, the Front Desk staff may give you information for hiring a third party babysitter.

Bars and Drinks

Would it surprise you to hear that there is a Disney-themed dive bar at the Disneyland Hotel and that it's *awesome*? Check out our recommendations of the best places to drink while at the Disneyland Resort:

Trader Sam's Enchanted Tiki Bar - *Top Choice!*
Location: Disneyland Hotel (pool area)
Description: Island-themed dive bar
Price: $$
Why We Recommend It: Dim lighting, air conditioning, and scraggly bartenders serve excellent drinks and bar food in this unique setting. Try a specialty cocktail or order a beer on draft. Certain drinks cause the room's volcanoes to erupt or brew a storm.
★ **Magic Tip** ★ After 8pm, Trader Sam's is 21 and older only.

Cove Bar - *Top Choice!*
Location: Disney California Adventure, Paradise Pier
Description: Casual Lounge with a full bar and extensive wine selection
Price: $$
Why We Recommend It: A great place to take it easy and enjoy a specialty cocktail or glass of wine while inside of the park. The Cove Bar is outdoors but covered, and has excellent views of the boardwalk with the California Scream' Rollercoaster.
★ **Magic Tip** ★ Get there early to avoid lines. The Cove Bar is a popular destination, but before 11.30am, you can have a great snack of Lobster Nachos or other bar food and start drinking without the lines.

Napa Rose Lounge
Location: Disney's Grand California Hotel and Spa

Description: Casual Lounge with a full bar and extensive wine selection
Price: $$
Why We Recommend It: A wine-lover's Disneyland dream! The Napa Rose Lounge is perfect for taking a break from the rides as you sit back and relax while you sip wine or nibble on excellent appetizers.

The Lounge at Steakhouse 55
Location: Disneyland Hotel
Description: Casual Lounge with a full bar and extensive wine selection
Price: $$
Why We Recommend It: The casual lounge and bar of the Disneyland Hotel. It's much cleaner and nicer than Trader Sam's, but serves its Disney charm with mouthwatering appetizers and a full bar with wine selections.

Carthay Circle Lounge
Location: Disney California Adventure, Buena Vista Street
Description: Casual Lounge with a full bar and extensive wine selection.
Price: $$
Why We Recommend It: A great place to take it easy and enjoy a specialty cocktail or glass of wine while inside the park.

Pacific Wharf Distribution Co.
Location: Disney California Adventure, Pacific Wharf
Description: A stand with an assortment of craft beers.
Price: $
Why We Recommend It: Order a beer that you can carry with you around the park (you must finish it before you get on a ride, but you can wait in line with it).
★ **Magic Tip** ★ The line can look long, but the servers pour fast so you won't be waiting long.

Rita's Baja Blenders
Location: Disney California Adventure, Pacific Wharf
Description: A stand with delicious margaritas and sangria.
Price: $
Why We Recommend It: Order a drink that you can carry with you around the park (you must finish it before you get on a ride, but you can wait in line with it).
★ **Magic Tip** ★ For a double shot of tequila, ask for the Grand Margarita.

Wine Country Trattoria
Location: Disney California Adventure, Pacific Wharf
Description: Wine and wine flights on a terrace.
Price: $$
Why We Recommend It: Excellent wine and magnificent views of Pacific Wharf.
★ **Magic Tip** ★ Book a World of Color package and drink wine before watching the show from reserved seating (book at Disneyland.com or call 714-781-3463).

ESPN Zone (Bar)
Location: Downtown Disney
Description: Sports Bar with a full menu
Price: $$
Why We Recommend It: Choose from a full bar with beer on draft while you watch sports on one of 120 HD screens.

Restaurants with Alcohol

Disney California Adventure

Alfresco Tasting Terrace - Disney Family of Wines.
Ariel's Grotto - full bar, specialty cocktails, and draft beers.
Bayside Brews - craft beer on draft and wine.
Carthay Circle Lounge - full bar with specialty cocktails
Carthay Circle Restaurant - Disney Family of Wines and cocktails.
Cove Bar - full bar, specialty cocktails, beer, and wine.
Mendocino Terrace - large selections of wines and domestic beer.
Sonoma Terrace - wine and craft beer selection.
Wine Country Trattoria - wine and wine flights, cocktails, sangria, and domestic beer.

Downtown Disney

Catal Restaurant - Wine, specialty cocktails, draft and bottled beers.
Crossroads at House of Blues® - Wines, bottled and draft beers.
ESPN Zone - Full bar and beer on draft
La Brea Bakery Café - Wines, bottled and draft beers.
Naples Ristorante e Pizzeria - Specialty cocktails, wines, and domestic beer.
Rainforest Cafe - Wines and domestic beer.
Ralph Brennan's Jazz Kitchen® - Specialty cocktails.
Tortilla Jo's - Specialty Margaritas, beer, specialty cocktails, and wines.
Uva Bar - A full bar with an extensive beer and wine list and specialty cocktails.

Disneyland Park

The are no options here. Disney kept it this way to keep Walt's vision alive for a family-friendly park.

How to Avoid Children

Okay, it's impossible to see absolutely no children at the Disneyland Resort, but you can avoid being around the bulk of them. We've listed some great tips on how to stay clear of families with small children at the parks.

Note: We've noticed that children 10 and older are generally very well-behaved at Disneyland. You may not even notice them as they are excited and stimulated by the sights just like you will be. Nevertheless, as promised, the tips:

1. Visit Trader Sam's Enchanted Tiki Bar after 8PM – no one under 21 is allowed in Trader Sam's after 8PM. You can drink from a full bar, eat, and lounge in this dive bar located in the Disneyland Hotel pool area (non-guests are allowed).

2. Stay Away from Fantasyland and Mickey's Toon Town – these kid-friendly lands are typically filled with small children. If you'd like to avoid them, we recommend staying away at all costs. However, the Matterhorn Bobsleds are great (the height restriction keeps the tiny children at bay).

3. Say "no" to Parades – these attractions are like magnets for small children. You've been warned.

4. Ride During a Parade – if you must ride a Fantasyland attraction, these are the best times! The families will flock to the parade route, generally leaving adults behind to wait for these popular rides. Check your park map for parade times.

5. Eat at a Bar – The Cove Bar in California and Carthay Circle Lounge are two of many places in Disney California Adventure that are generally kid-free (or have far fewer children than other places).

6. Eat at the Blue Bayou (Disneyland) – This table service restaurant is generally quiet and kid-free. Don't forget to make a reservation before you go!

7. Don't enter "a bug's land" (Disney California Adventure) – this is the kid-friendly zone that will make any child-avoiding adult cringe.

8. Attractions to Avoid:

   In Disneyland
   - Astro Orbiter
   - Autopia
   - Buzz Lightyear Astro Blaster
   - Fantasyland
   - Finding Nemo Submarine Voyage
   - Mickey's Toon Town
   - The Many Adventures of Winnie the Pooh
   - Tarzan's Treehouse
   - Pirate's Lair on Tom Sawyer Island

   In Disney California Adventure
   - "a bug's land"

- Golden Zephyr
- Goofy's Sky School
- Jumpin' Jellyfish
- King Triton's Carousel
- The Little Mermaid
- Monsters, Inc. Mike & Sulley to the Rescue!
- Red Car Trolley
- Redwood Creek Challenge Trial
- Silly Symphony Swings
- *Turtle Talk with Crush*

9. Stay away from Redd Rocket's Pizza Port in Tomorrowland. This place is typically filled with kids eager to run around tables while they devour pizza.

10. Pay attention to height requirements because children are generally small, these restrictions can instantly weed them out at the start of the queue.

Downtown Disney for Adults

There are many things to do in Downtown Disney that adults will love, from movies to shopping and even seeing a rock concert or a live DJ!

1. **Watch a Movie** - AMC Theatres offers a wide selection of movies. Visit www.amctheatres.com for show times.
2. **Go Shopping** - Buy surf gear at Quicksilver or makeup at Sephora.
3. **Lounge at Starbucks** - With free Wi-Fi and drink favorites you can spend time on their massive patio as people stroll by.

4. **See a Free Concert** - Musicians love Downtown Disney. They rent the stages and booths to perform nightly concerts.
5. **Go Bowling** - Splitsville comes to Downtown Disney in the Fall/Winter 2017!

Smoking Sections

There are a total of 5 smoking areas at the Disneyland Parks and 6 near the Disneyland Hotels. Also, the Disneyland Resort considers e-cigarettes to be "smoking". Downtown Disney allows smoking but with restrictions (see next page).

Note:
During Mickey's Halloween Party (a separate event held September through October, the will not be any smoking inside of the park. Instead, you will have to leave to the esplanade (the space between the two parks) to smoke and re-enter when you have finished.

Disneyland Smoking
1. Main Entry Plaza - The esplanade between Disneyland and Disney California Adventure.
2. Tomorrowland - Look for this section near Autopia and the train station.
3. Frontierland - Almost directly across from The Haunted Mansion.

Disney California Adventure Smoking
1. Hollywood Land - Look for the area near the Monsters, Inc. ride.
2. Grizzly Peak - Follow the trail behind the Grizzly River Run.

Disneyland Hotel Smoking
1. Adventure Tower – On the southeast corner.
2. Fantasy Tower – On the northwest corner.
3. Frontier Tower – On the south side.

Disney's Grand Californian Hotel and Spa
1. Outdoor – Near the Hearthstone Lounge.
2. Courtyard – On the opposite side of Sephora, inside of the hotel courtyard.

Disney's Paradise Pier Hotel
The closest smoking section is the Frontier Tower at the Disneyland Hotel (located on the south side).

Downtown Disney
You make smoke in Downtown Disney, but not in the restrooms, stores, or near the restaurants.

Chapter Fifteen
A Non-Rider's Guide

Introduction

Typically, the first thing that people think about at Disneyland is the castle. The second thought is usually the rides. But what if you or your guest don't enjoy the drops, turns, and twists. Are there things for you to do? Would you enjoy yourself? Would it be worth the money? In short, is the Disneyland Resort for you? The answer is: YES! The attractions at the resort aren't all rides. In fact, most of them are shows, sights to see, activities, and more that are accessible by everyone! Disneyland and Disney California Adventure are sure to offer something for everyone.

Recommendations:

• See the sights - Disneyland and Disney California Adventure are something to behold. They offer intricate architecture, well-planned lands, and lush, meticulously manicured foliage.
• Eat gourmet food - Dazzle your senses with savory meals and sweet treats all around the parks, hotels, and Downtown Disney.
• See a show - The Disneyland Resort is known for magnificent shows and parades
• Meet Characters - Take a photo with your favorite Disney character. Or watch the many musical bands playing around the park.
• Ride a slow-moving attraction - Some rides don't have drops or move fast, many of them can be perfect for your speed as you experience the magnificent stories these rides have to offer.
• Shop! - There are stores on every corner of the parks.
• Get a Princess Makeover at the Bibbidi Bobbidi Boutique - perfect for kids who want to dress as their favorite Disney Princess.
• People Watch - this will either sound fun or creepy to you, but Disneyland has some unique visitors in creative outfits, or watch them plummet from Splash Mountain!

Most Recommended Shows and Parades to Watch (in order):

1. World of Color (Disney California Adventure)
2. "Fantasy In The Sky" Fireworks (Disneyland)
3. Paint the Night Parade (Disneyland)
4. Jedi Training (Disneyland)
5. Fantasy Faire (Disneyland)
6. Mickey and the Magical Map (Disneyland)
7. Laughing Stock Co. (Disneyland)
8. See the Disney classic, *Steamboat Willie* at the Main Street Cinema (Disneyland).

Best of the Slow Rides and Attractions

These attractions don't have drops or move quickly at all. Here are some you may enjoy (in order):

1. Explore the Disney Animation Building (Disney California Adventure) – learn to draw and see how the animators bring Disney classics to life!
2. Heimlich's Chew Chew Train (Disney California Adventure) – a slow-moving train with humor and delicious aromas.
3. Peter Pan's Flight (Disneyland) – see the story of *Peter Pan* while flying in a slow-moving pirate ship.
4. Jungle Cruise (Disneyland) – a humorous tour guide takes you on a riverboat through the Amazon and Africa.
5. Alice in Wonderland (Disneyland) – a classic "dark ride" through the story of Disney's *Alice in Wonderland*.
6. The Little Mermaid – Ariel's Undersea Adventure (Disney California Adventure) – a slow-moving "dark ride" that explores the story of Disney's *The Little Mermaid*.
7. Haunted Mansion (Disneyland) – a slow-moving "dark ride" through a haunted house.
8. "it's a small world" (Disneyland) – the classic, slow-paced boat ride around the world.

Other Fun without Rides

- Order a pair of customized Mickey Ears with your name on them (Disneyland)
- Try to lift the sword in the stone (Disneyland – Fantasyland, near the carousel)
- Check out the Disney Gallery on Main Street, U.S.A. (Disneyland)
- Look for Push the Talking Trashcan (Disneyland – Tomorrowland)
- Play the Fun Wheel Challenge right before World of Color (Disney California Adventure)
- Watch the Dapper Dans, a barbershop quartet, perform on Main Street, U.S.A. (Disneyland)
- Look at the vegetables that grow in Tomorrowland (Disneyland)
- Book a backstage tour and see how the magic is created. Call (714) 781-8687.

Chapter Sixteen
FastPass® and Single Rider Line Locations

Disneyland FastPass® Locations

Big Thunder Mountain Railroad – To the right of the regular line in Frontierland.
Necessity: Medium

Haunted Mansion – To the left of the ride line gates in New Orleans Square.
Necessity: Low

Indiana Jones Adventure – Between the ride line and Jungle Cruise in Adventureland.
Necessity: High

Matterhorn Bobsleds – Coming later in 2017.
Necessity: Likely Medium

Roger Rabbit's Car Toon Spin - At the FastPass sign near the ride in Mickey's Toontown.
Necessity: Low

Space Mountain (Hyperspace Mountain) - To the right of the regular queue in Tomorrowland. Sometimes there is a separate line for the FastPass, hold close to the right side.
Necessity: High

Splash Mountain - Across from The Many Adventures of Winnie the Pooh in Critter Country.
Necessity: High (Low on cold days)

Star Tours: The Adventures Continue - Across from the queue, next to Buzz Lightyear Astro Blasters in Tomorrowland.
Necessity: Medium

California Adventure FastPass Locations:

California Screamin' - To the left of the queue in Paradise Pier.
Necessity: Medium

Guardians of the Galaxy – Mission: Breakout - Coming Early Summer 2017. Across from ride queue in Hollywood Land.
Necessity: Likely Very High

Goofy's Sky School - To the right of the queue in Paradise Pier.
Necessity: Low

Grizzly River Run - To the left of the queue in Grizzly Peak.
Necessity: Medium (High on hot days, Low on cold days)

Radiator Springs Racers - Near *It's Tough to be a Bug!* in "a bug's land". Sometimes the FastPass line will continue into Buena Vista Street, especially on busier days.
Necessity: High

Soarin' - To the left the queue in Grizzly Peak.
Necessity: Medium

Toy Story Midway Mania - Coming later in 2017.
Necessity: Likely High

World of Color - Look for the kiosks near the Grizzly River Run in Grizzly Peak.
Necessity: High

Disneyland Single Rider Line Locations:

Indiana Jones Adventure - Ask the cast member at the queue start for a Single Rider pass.
Necessity: Medium

Splash Mountain - This is a bit hidden and located by walking through the exit of the ride until you reach a cast member to ask about the Single Rider Line.
Necessity: High

Matterhorn Bobsleds - Ask a cast member at the line exit for the Single Rider Line.
Necessity: Low

California Adventure Single Rider Line Locations:

California Screamin' – Another hidden line (though it's marked with a blue sign) located by walking through the left side of the queue where you will see a gate (it takes you to the opposite side of the rollercoaster boarding)
Necessity: Medium

Soarin' Over California – At the FastPass entrance, ask a cast member for the Single Rider Line.
Necessity: Medium

Grizzly River Run – Move up the exit stairs and meet the cast members at the rotating platform to ask about the Single Rider Line.
Necessity: Medium (High on hot days, Low on cold days)

Radiator Springs Racers – A clearly marked queue at the start of the queues.
Necessity: High

Goofy's Sky School – Look for the yellow sign near the start of the queue and by the FastPass line.
Necessity: Low

Chapter Seventeen
Tips for Getting Free Stuff

Introduction

You can get some great souvenirs and treats for free at the Disneyland Resort. Of course, you still have to pay for your ticket, but these are great things that you can eat, take home with you, or use along the way.

List of Free Items:

Maps
This might be obvious, but it's a great souvenir, especially since they have the surrounding dates of your arrival. These are located at the entrances to Disneyland and Disney California Adventure.

Chocolate
Get a free chocolate square when you enter (Disney California Adventure).

Special Occasion Pin
Celebrate your birthday, anniversary, and more with a free pin (Disneyland, and no they don't card you on your birthday).

Boudin Bread
During the Boudin Factory Tour each guest receives a free piece of sample bread (Disney California Adventure).

Disney Art
Learn to draw your favorite Disney characters from and keep the paper at the Animation Academy in Disney California Adventure.

Stickers
Take a survey near the entrance to the parks and ask for a sticker.

Professional Photos
Stop at any of the photo booths scattered around the park and ask the Disneyland photographer to take a photo with your camera. They are happy to do so and typically they do a great job! (Disneyland and Disney California Adventure)

Extra FastPasses
If you have an interest in the Disney Vacation Club (or even if you don't), they offer three free FastPasses to each person in your group for watching the 60-90-minute presentation. These can be used at either park for any ride except the Radiator Springs Racers. (Downtown Disney)

Chapter Eighteen
The Best of the Disneyland Resort: Top 8 Lists

Introduction

The Disneyland Resort has seemingly endless attractions, sights, and food to enjoy. We can understand if you feel overwhelmed deciding what to do! Don't worry because we're coming to the rescue with our most recommended things to do during your stay at Disneyland:

Listed in Order
(#1 being the most recommended)

Best Thrill Rides
1. Space Mountain (Disneyland)
2. Tower of Terror (Disney California Adventure)
3. Indiana Jones Adventure (Disneyland)

4. Radiator Springs Racers (Disney California Adventure)
5. Splash Mountain (Disneyland)
6. California Screamin' Rollercoaster (Disney California Adventure)
7. Big Thunder Mountain Railroad (Disneyland)
8. Star Tours - The Adventures Continue (Disneyland)

Best Family Rides
1. Toy Story Midway Mania (Disney California Adventure)
2. Pirates of the Caribbean (Disneyland)
3. Peter Pan's Flight (Disneyland)
4. Mad Tea Party (Disneyland)
5. Haunted Mansion: Holiday (Disneyland)
6. Mater's Junkyard Jamboree (Disney California Adventure)
7. Jungle Cruise (Disneyland)
8. Dumbo the Flying Elephant (Disneyland)

Best Slow-Moving Rides for Kids
1. Peter Pan's Flight (Disneyland)
2. Heimlich's Chew Chew Train (Disney California Adventure)
3. Toy Story Midway Mania! (Disney California Adventure)
4. Mad Tea Party (Disneyland)
5. Alice in Wonderland (Disneyland)
6. The Little Mermaid (Disney California Adventure)
7. Dumbo the Flying Elephant (Disneyland)
8. The Many Adventures of Winnie the Pooh (Disneyland)

Best Non-Ride Attractions
1. *It's Tough to be a Bug!* (Disney California Adventure)
2. Animation Academy (Disney California Adventure)
3. *Turtle Talk with Crush* (Disney California Adventure)
4. Sorcerer's Workshop (Disney California Adventure)
5. The Bakery Tour (Disney California Adventure)
6. Enchanted Tiki Room (Disneyland)

7. Strolling Mickey's Toontown (Disneyland)
8. Sleeping Beauty Castle Walkthrough (Disneyland)

Best Food
1. Monte Cristo Sandwich (Disneyland - Blue Bayou Restaurant and Café Orleans)
2. Dole Whip (Disneyland - Tiki Juice Bar)
3. Lobster Nachos (Disney California Adventure, Cove Bar)
4. Churros (Disneyland and Disney California Adventure)
5. Corndog (Disneyland Little Red Wagon Corn Dogs and Disney California Adventure Corn Dog Castle)
6. Clam Chowder in a Sourdough Bread Bowl (Disneyland, French Market Restaurant - California Adventure, Pacific Wharf Café)
7. Lobster Roll (Disneyland, Harbour Galley)
8. Chili Cheese Dog - a hot dog with a delicious spread of chili sauce (Disneyland, Refreshment Corner)

Note: Look for the *"Top Choice!"* in the restaurant descriptions for our most recommended.

Best Fun for Disney Princess Fans
1. Bibbidi Bobbidi Boutique (Disneyland)
2. Royal Hall (Disneyland)
3. The Little Mermaid: Ariel's Undersea Adventure (Disney California Adventure)
4. The Royal Theatre (Disneyland)
5. Sleeping Beauty's Castle (Disneyland)
6. Pixie Hollow (Disneyland)
7. Mickey's Soundsational Parade –features Ariel, Tianna, Cinderella, Snow White, Aurora, Belle, and Rapunzel (Disneyland)
8. Frozen: Live at the Hyperion (Disney California Adventure)

Best Magic Tips:
1. Follow Our Pre-Planned Ride Guides
2. Book Your Restaurant Reservation Early - Disneyland.com or call (714) 781-DINE.
3. Win at Buzz Lightyear Blasters - shoot the target on Emperor Zurg's chest toward the end for 50,000 points a hit (Disneyland, Tomorrowland).
4. Win at Toy Story Midway Mania - shoot the volcano lava in Trixie and Dixie's play screen to unleash an explosion of 500 point balloons (Disney California Adventure, Paradise Pier).
5. Rent a Locker
6. Get the Radiator Spring Racers FastPass
7. Take a Selfie on Tarzan's Treehouse™
8. Pirates of the Caribbean Shortest Line - the right side has less queue!

Chapter Nineteen
Hidden Mickeys

Introduction

It's no secret that Walt Disney loved his cartoon mouse, Mickey. Ever since he created the character in the 1920's, Mickey has found his way into nearly every piece of Walt Disney's creations from films to logos to them parks. Now, you might be thinking *Mickey Mouse isn't in Cinderella or Aladdin!* – where, in fact, he is- or, at least, his image is. You know that famous logo of the Mickey ears? It's just three circles, a large one for the face and two smaller ones for the ears. Well, these show up *everywhere* from the bubbles while Cinderella scrubbed the floors during her labors to a quick scene where Jasmine's pet tiger, Raja, changes briefly into a Mickey-like head. Even *Frozen* has a Mickey doll in a bookcase in one of the scenes. But like we said, Mickey doesn't just show up in the films- he's also all over the parks. These often hard-to-spot images of him are called "Hidden Mickeys" because, well, they're hidden!

But why? Think of Hidden Mickeys as a nod to Walt, the spirit of the Parks, and as a special treat for the guests. Finding Hidden Mickeys is a fun way to pass the time waiting in the decorated queues. In this exciting chapter, we reveal dozens of Hidden Mickeys in the Parks and Downtown Disney!

Disneyland

1. Adventureland – On the Jungle Cruise, check out a cast iron pan with a familiar shape inside of it.
2. Adventureland – Tarzan's Treehouse has a very cool Hidden Mickey made of rope. Look for it holding up a curtain.
3. Adventureland – The Adventureland Bazaar is home to a Hidden Mickey. Look for a Mickey head on a wall inside of a wooden circle.
4. Adventureland – The Indiana Jones Adventure has a Mickey hidden in its hieroglyphs on the well. This one is hard to spot!

5. Critter Country – While waiting in line for Splash Mountain, look in the barn to see crank gears in the shape of a Mickey head.
6. Critter Country – One of the tree knots on Splash Mountain's warning sign has a Hidden Mickey. This one is a bit hard to find!
7. Critter Country – The Briar Patch Gift Shop has a Mickey-shaped lettuce head on a shelf.
8. Critter Country – In the Many Adventures of Winnie the Pooh ride, look for a Mickey hat near Pooh's honey bottles as he falls asleep in his room.

9. Fantasyland – The Village Haus restaurant has a Hidden Mickey painted in gold on the back of a model ship.
10. Fantasyland – On the Alice in Wonderland ride, keep your eyes open for a hidden Mickey in red pain splashed on one of the Queen's hedges.
11. Fantasyland – While climbing aboard a Storybook Land Canal Boat, look for Hidden Mickeys painted on the floral designs.
12. Fantasyland – When starting the wait for Peter Pan's Flight, look up to a window with toys. A Hidden Mickey is located in the teddy bear's paw.
13. Fantasyland – On King Arthur's Carousel, a horse named Jingles has three jewels in the shape of a Mickey head.
14. Fantasyland – When waiting in line for to meet Tinker Bell in Pixie Hollow, looking for the "Fairies Welcome" sign. On the post, you'll see a Mickey head carving.
15. Fantasyland – Mr. Toad's Wild Ride has a Hidden Mickey in the corner of the stained glass window. You'll see this door right after the suit of armor falls.
16. Fantasyland – Look for a wooden Mickey head at the top of the pirate ship in Pinocchio's Daring Journey toward the end of the ride.

17. Frontierland – The Golden Horseshoe stage has a Hidden Mickey in one of the vents at the bottom of the stage.
18. Frontierland – At the top of the Mark Twain Riverboat, look for a Mickey head in the iron bars next to the smokestacks.
19. Frontierland – In the Rancho del Zocalo Restaurante, look for a Hidden Mickey near the condiments.
20. Frontierland – On Big Thunder Mountain, look for three large gears that are shaped like a Mickey head.

21. Main Street, U.S.A. – In City Hall, look for a painting with Mickey Mouse holding a child's hand. On the other side is a man in a white t-shirt. On the back of his shirt is a Hidden Mickey.
22. Main Street, U.S.A. – In the Main Street Magic Shop, a Hidden Mickey is made out of white trick rope in a display case.
23. Main Street, U.S.A. – If you wander the corners of Main Street, you'll see the Disneyland Casting Agency. The sign for the agency has two Hidden Mickeys at the top and one at the bottom, made of gold leaf.
24. Main Street, U.S.A. – The Market House has an iron decoration with Mickeys around the rim.

25. New Orleans Square – The famous Blue Bayou restaurant has stained glass in its lobby. Look to the top and spot three circles of glass in the shape of a Mickey head.
26. New Orleans Square – During the Haunted Mansion, look for the ballroom scene with the ghosts. On a table, there are three plates together in the shape of Mickey's head.
27. New Orleans Square – Pirates of the Caribbean has a difficult-to-spot Hidden Mickey in the final area. As the pirates fire shots at one another, look to the left for a gold armor hanging on the walls behind the barrels of explosives. In the center of the gold armor chest plate is a Hidden Mickey.
28. New Orleans Square – When you first splash down in Pirate of the Caribbean, look for a beach with crabs. You'll spot three shells in the sand in the shape of a Mickey head.

29. Toontown – The Fireworks Factory has a pink firework coming out of the red brick. Look for a blue Hidden Mickey painted on it.
30. Toontown – Mickey's House has a Hidden Mickey in the projector screen. The countdown circle has two black ears.
31. Toontown – In Minnie's House, look for a Hidden Mickey on a book between *Little Mouse of the Prairie* and *Cheese and Remembrance*.
32. Toontown – The lamp between Mickey's House and Chip 'n' Dale Treehouse has Hidden Mickeys.

33. Tomorrowland – Little Green Men Store Command, when you exit Buzz Lightyear's Astro Blasters, has a Hidden Mickey surrounded by rings at the top of the displays.
34. Tomorrowland – The speakers for Space Mountain on the seats are in the shape of a Hidden Mickey.
35. Tomorrowland – When in line for Star Tours – The Adventures Continue, look for a Hidden Mickey on C-3PO's top display monitor.
36. Tomorrowland – Buzz Lightyear's Astro Blasters has a hidden Mickey on the Scrabble-like wooden blocks in the first room.

Disney California Adventure

37. Buena Vista Street – The Five & Dime Band's car has Hidden Mickeys on the tire rubber.
38. Buena Vista Street – The black alarm bell in Oswald's Filling Station is has Mickey ears.
39. Buena Vista Street – Elias & Company's men's department has iron bars in the shape of Mickey heads.

40. Buena Vista Street – Julius Katz & Sons display window has Mickey-shaped watch parts.

41. a bug's land – The beverage stand that serves Fanta has cherries in the shape of a Mickey head.
42. a bug's land – Flik's Flyers have a Hidden Mickey in the concrete where the circular metal plates line together.
43. a bug's land – It's Tough to be a Bug! has three mushrooms that line up to look like a Mickey head. They are located to the left of the stage and a bit hard to find.
44. a bug's land – At the end of Heimlich's Chew Chew Train, look for a rock wall with three stones that appear to be a Hidden Mickey.

45. Cars Land – In the line for Radiator Springs Racers, look for three circular cactus in the shape of Mickey's head.
46. Cars Land – The Radiator Springs Racers have a Hidden Mickey in the projections on the walls when the tractors tip.
47. Cars Land – Look for a Mickey in the paint on the red tool shed with wheels right after Guido's Casa Della Tires.
48. Cars Land – Mater's Junkyard Jamboree has a Hidden Mickey made of hubcaps in the top corner of the queue.

49. Grizzly Peak – During Soarin' Around the World, look for three hot air balloons to make a Hidden Mickey.

50. Hollywood Land – Outside of the Animation Building, look for a Mickey Head at the top of the flagpole.
51. Hollywood Land – If you're looking for an easy-to-spot Mickey, go into the Sorcerer's Workshop in the

Animation Building. There, you'll spot Mickey-shaped balloons at the drawing station.
52. Hollywood Land – In the line for Monsters Inc. Mike & Sulley to the Rescue! look for the yellow cabs in the artwork on the televisions that have upside down Hidden Mickeys near the grill.
53. Hollywood Land – The Monsters Inc. ride also has a furry Sulley animatronic where he has a purple spot in the shape of Mickey's head on his bottom.

54. Paradise Pier – The Little Mermaid ~ Ariel's Undersea Adventure has a Hidden Mickey in the shape of barnacles on the mural when loading into the clam shells.
55. Paradise Pier – The pole of the Jumpin' Jellyfish has a Hidden Mickey painted on it.
56. Paradise Pier – Goofy's Sky School has a Hidden Mickey on the wrench toward the exit.
57. Paradise Pier – Toy Story Midway Mania has Jessie and friends in three circles that make up a Hidden Mickey. Spot this when you're loading for the ride.

Downtown Disney

58. D Street – The brick wall covered in art is in the shape of a Hidden Mickey.
59. Something Silver – There is a mosaic swirl that is easy to spot.

World of Disney – This store is almost a literal gold mine of Hidden Mickeys. Scan the murals to the statues to the railings for Hidden Mickey. To start, look for the blue Mickey head at the top of the World of Disney sign.

Chapter Twenty
Disneyland Legends

Introduction

Over the past 60 years, The Disneyland Resort has garnered its share of legends and myths. Some speak of cats roaming the grounds at night while others worry about ghosts that come out after dark. Could any of these be true? You might be surprised to know that many of these myths are heavily based in reality. In fact, some of the craziest myths of them all could be completely true! While many of the rumors might just be material of the imagination, we'll pick them apart and tell you the fact. This section contains a list of some of the most popular myths surrounding the Disneyland Park.

Disneyland Park Legends

Haunted Mansion Death Certificate
The Legend: At the end of the Haunted Mansion ride, ask for a "death certificate". These are given out only rarely and to certain guests.
Reality: Fiction.
Notes: Contrary to what many believe, there never has been a "death certificate" and any you find on the internet are not authentic.

Jungle Cruise Maps
The Legend: At the end of the Jungle Cruse ride, ask for a free map.
Reality: Fact!
Notes: Unlike the "death certificate", this one was real! After unloading from the Jungle Cruise boat, you once could ask a cast member for a free map. Sadly, these no longer seem to be available (though it still may be worth asking as Disneyland will only silently bring back treasures like these).

Pirates of the Caribbean Skull
The Legend: In the ride, on the headboard of the treasures room is a real skull and bones. Some of these bones were taken from the UCLA Medical Center.
Reality: Likely Fiction.
Notes: While it's crazy to think that a real person's bones could be buried inside of the ride, it appears that this is a work of fiction. We believe if there is any fact in it, the bones may have been cast from actual ones, but they are not real. However, Disneyland hasn't confirmed this, so we may never truly know!

Disneyland Birth
The Legend: If a child is born in the park, he or she will get a lifetime membership to Disneyland.
Reality: Fiction.
Notes: In 1979, a baby girl was accidently born at Disneyland (the first person ever born at the park). However, it remains just a myth that she was ever given a free lifetime membership to the park. She did, however, get her photo taken with Mickey and his friends! Expectant mothers are advised to induce labor elsewhere.
Fact: Since its opening, 4 babies have been born at the Disneyland Resort. All of them have been girls!

Club 33: Disneyland's Private Club
The Legend: There is a very exclusive club in Disneyland with gourmet chefs and alcohol.
Reality: Fact!
Notes: Club 33 is very real and you can see the door to the right of the Blue Bayou in New Orleans Square (though the entrance is a bit further down). However, it is very exclusive and you have to be invited to dine or drink there. If you know someone with a membership, they can allow you inside by reserving you on the guest list. The initiation fee is $25,000 plus dues of $10,000/year and the waiting list is *years* long. Club 33 members get loads of benefits from free park tickets to sneak peaks.
For more information, visit: www.disneylandclub33.com (not an official website).

The Matterhorn Basketball Court
The Legend: Inside of the Matterhorn is a half basketball court.
Reality: Fact!
Notes: Designed for the climbers of the Matterhorn in their spare time, the basketball court is a small stress reliever. Unfortunately, this is not open to guests.

Disneyland Dream Suite
The Legend: There is a magical, princess-themed suite in the Disneyland Resort that allows guests to stay overnight inside of the park!
Reality: Fact!
Notes: During certain contest times, Disneyland gives away free stays in the Dream Suite above Pirates of the Caribbean.
There are signs pointing to the suite located in New Orleans Square.

Tomorrowland Edible Plants
The Legend: All of the plants are edible.
Reality: Fact!
Notes: Look for beautiful cabbages, herbs, cornstalks, and fruit trees all over Tomorrowland. The area's theme is a "space colony", hence why the plants might need to be edible in the future. While not every part of these plants are edible, they could be trees that bear fruit. Disneyland doesn't recommend that you eat these plants, so please admire them without touching.

Disneyland Cats
The Legend: Disneyland is home to dozens of cats that roam the grounds at night.
Reality: Fact!
Notes: Cats indeed run about the park and sometimes you can see them wandering at night! The cats are well-fed and encouraged to stay there to keep down the population of rats that might otherwise infiltrate the park. During the day, the cats go behind the scenes to rest up before starting their late-night prowling.

"Andy's Coming!"
The Legend: If you yell "Andy's coming!" to the costumed characters of Pixar's *Toy Story*, they will all instantly drop and freeze.
Reality: No longer Fact
Notes: Video on the internet suggests that this was once true, however, they don't do this anymore. It's not recommended to yell "Andy's Coming" at the characters as it won't work.

Walt's Apartment
The Legend: Walt Disney kept a private apartment in the Disneyland Park.
Reality: Fact!
Notes: You can see it on Main Street, U.S.A., just above the firehouse. Backstage tours will often guide inside of this space that is now a small museum dedicated to the visionary.
To book a tour, call (714) 781-8687.

Disneyland Ghosts
The Legend: Close to a dozen ghosts haunt the grounds of Disneyland after the guests have gone home.
Reality: Unconfirmed
Notes: It depends what you believe, but many cast members have reported seeing strange apparitions late at night after the guests have gone. Disneyland attempts to keep these ghost stories alive to entertain guest. For instance, they posted a video on YouTube showing a cast member in the former Twilight Zone™ Tower of Terror ride and a ghostly figure flicking in an empty seat. However, it was later discovered to be a thing of Disney magic.

Tattoos are Banned from Disneyland
The Legend: Guests must cover up all tattoos before entering the park.

Reality: Fiction
Notes: Though magazines have published that Disneyland bans tattoos, this is completely false. In fact, you'll see many, many guests with tattoos from head to toe - many of them Disney related! The only rule is that tattoos that are offensive or contain nudity must be concealed.

Walt Disney is Frozen
The Legend: Walt Disney is cryogenically frozen at the Disneyland Park and will be reanimated in the future when he can be cured.
Reality: Fiction
Notes: Walt Disney was a private man, so the public wasn't privy to the details surrounding his death. However, Walt's grave is located in Glendale California.

$1 Tickets
The Legend: When Disneyland first opened, an adult ticket was just $1.
Reality: Fact!
Notes: It's true that when the Disneyland Park first opened in 1955, admission for an adult was only a buck! Even crazier was that kids were just 50 cents each. Now, you might argue that with inflation that's not a big variance. However, it's not! $1 in 1955 works out to $8.85 in 2017. Considering that an average Disneyland ticket is over $100, that's a huge pricing difference (also keep in mind that there are many more attractions these days).

Chapter Twenty-One
Pre-Planned Ride and Attraction Lists

Want to avoid long lines and enjoy your day more? These pre-planned guides proven to just do that! Whether you are there for days on end or trying to get to both parks in one day, we have you covered. Review these lists and have fun!

★ **Magic Tips** ★
1. Get to the park early and grab a map at the entrance.
2. Take a photo of ride list you've chosen with your phone or cut it out to take with you.
3. Make all of your lunch and dinner before arrival.
4. Take a break when you need to in between rides.
5. Keep calm, enjoy the sights, and take in the magical feelings of The Happiest Place on Earth!

Note: Your FastPass may not sync with our suggested time. You may have to switch a ride placement if this happens.

Disneyland

Thrill Riders

1. **Space Mountain FastPass** (Tomorrowland)
   The FastPass distribution is located to the right of the ride's queue. You won't ride Space Mountain just yet.
2. **Star Tours** (Tomorrowland)
3. **Buzz Lightyear Astro Blasters** (Tomorrowland)
4. **Matterhorn Bobsleds** (Fantasyland)
   Ask to the cast member if you can ride the left side rollercoaster (Tomorrowland side) for the faster speeds.
5. **Mad Tea Party** (Fantasyland)
6. **Sleeping Beauty Castle Walkthrough** (Fantasyland)
7. **Space Mountain** (Tomorrowland)
   use your FastPass
8. **Star Wars Launch Bay** (Tomorrowland)
   Meet the cuddly Chewbacca or the scary Kylo Ren
9. **Indiana Jones Adventure FastPass** (Adventureland)
10. **Jungle Cruise** (Adventureland)
11. **Splash Mountain** (Critter Country)
12. **The Haunted Mansion** (New Orleans Square)
13. **Big Thunder Mountain Railroad** (Frontierland)
14. **Pirates of the Caribbean** (Adventureland)
15. **Indiana Jones Adventure** (Adventureland)
    use your FastPass
16. **Disneyland Fireworks** (Main Street, U.S.A.)

Still have more time? Ride your favorites again, hop on board a Disneyland classic like Peter Pan's Flight, or watch the Disneyland Fireworks show!

Classic Disneyland

1. **Space Mountain FastPass** (Tomorrowland)
   The FastPass distribution is located to the right of the ride's queue. You won't ride Space Mountain just yet.
2. **Star Tours** (Tomorrowland)
3. **Finding Nemo Submarine Voyage** (Tomorrowland)
4. **Matterhorn Bobsleds** (Tomorrowland)
5. **Peter Pan's Flight** (Fantasyland)
6. **Mad Tea Party** (Fantasyland)
7. **"it's a small world"** (Fantasyland)
8. **Mickey or Minnie's House** (Mickey's Toontown)
9. **Space Mountain** (Tomorrowland)
   use your FastPass
10. **Indiana Jones Adventure FastPass** (Adventureland)
11. **Jungle Cruise** (Adventureland)
12. **Pirates of the Caribbean** (New Orleans Square)
13. **The Haunted Mansion** (New Orleans Square)
14. **Indiana Jones Adventure** (Adventureland)
    use your FastPass
15. **Big Thunder Mountain Railroad** (Frontierland)
16. **Disneyland Fireworks** (Main Street, U.S.A.)

Still have more time? Ride your favorites again, hop on board a Disneyland classic like Peter Pan's Flight, or watch the Disneyland Fireworks show!

With Kids (Ages 6-10)

1. **Peter Pan's Flight** (Fantasyland)
2. **Dumbo the Flying Elephant** (Fantasyland)
3. **Gadget's Go-Coaster** (Mickey's Toontown)
4. **Roger Rabbit's Car Toon Spin** (Toontown)
5. **Mickey or Minnie's House** (Toontown)
6. **Mad Tea Party** (Fantasyland)
7. **Alice in Wonderland** (Fantasyland)
8. **Autopia FastPass** (Tomorrowland)
9. **Finding Nemo Submarine Voyage** (Tomorrowland)
10. **Buzz Lightyear Astro Blasters** (Tomorrowland)
11. **Star Wars Launch Bay** (Tomorrowland)
    Meet the cuddly Chewbacca or the scary Kylo Ren
12. **Autopia** (Tomorrowland)
    use your FastPass
13. **Tarzan's Treehouse™** (Adventureland)
14. **The Many Adventures of Winnie the Pooh** (Critter Country)
15. **Pirates of the Caribbean** (New Orleans Square)
16. **Paint the Night Parade** (Main Street, U.S.A.)
17. **Disneyland Fireworks** (Main Street, U.S.A.)

Notes: If your child enjoys faster rides, consider the following:
   a. Replace Alice in Wonderland (7) with The Matterhorn Bobsleds.
   b. Replace Autopia (8 for the FastPass and 11 for the ride) with Space Mountain.

With Young Kids (Ages 2-5)

1. *Peter Pan's Flight (Fantasyland)
2. *Dumbo the Flying Elephant (Fantasyland)
3. Storybook Land Canal Boats (Fantasyland)
4. Bibbidi Bobbidi Boutique (Fantasyland)
   or ride the Casey Jr. Circus Train
5. Fantasy Faire (Fantasyland)
   Meet a princess and/or see a short theatre show
6. Mickey or Minnie's House (Mickey's Toontown)
7. *Alice in Wonderland (Fantasyland)
8. *"it's a small world" (Fantasyland)
9. *Finding Nemo Submarine Voyage (Tomorrowland)
10. Mickey's Soundsational Parade (Main Street, U.S.A.)
11. Tarzan's Treehouse™ (Adventureland)
12. *The Many Adventures of Winnie the Pooh (Critter Country)
13. *Paint the Night Parade (Main Street, U.S.A.)
14. Disneyland Fireworks (Main Street, U.S.A.)

*Attractions we recommend the most for preschoolers.
We understand that a list like this may not be so cut and dry when it comes to dealing with a fickle preschool-aged child. We recommend spreading out each attraction, and if you're met with resistance, venture into a gift shop, grab a snack, or enjoy the sights of Disneyland – or head back to the hotel for a nap. Even if you only get the attractions with a * next to it, you've had a successful and memorable day!

Disney California Adventure

Thrill Riders

1. **Radiator Springs Racers FastPass** ("a bug's land")
   The FastPass distribution is located near "It's Tough to be a Bug!" (not in Cars Land). You won't ride the Racers just yet.
2. **World of Color FastPass** (Grizzly Peak)
   Distribution is located next to the Grizzly River Run. The World of Color FastPass™ won't affect or be affected by other passes.
3. **California Screamin'** (Paradise Pier)
4. **Toy Story Midway Mania®** (Paradise Pier)
5. **Mickey's Fun Wheel** (Paradise Pier)
6. **Silly Symphony Swings** (Paradise Pier)
7. **Goofy's Sky School** (Paradise Pier)
8. **Grizzly River Run** (Grizzly Peak)
   Skip this if you don't want to get wet.
9. **Soarin'** (Grizzly Peak)
10. **Animation Academy** (Hollywood Land)
11. **Radiator Springs Racers** (Cars Land)
    use your FastPass
12. **Mater's Junkyard Jamboree** (Cars Land)
13. ***It's Tough to be a Bug!*** ("a bug's land)
14. **World of Color** (Paradise Pier)

*Guardians of the Galaxy – Mission: Breakout will open in Spring/Summer 2017. Make sure you reserve a FastPass first thing, possibly instead of Radiator Springs Racers.

Have more time? Check out Monsters Inc. Mike and Sulley to the Rescue! (Hollywood Land) or Luigi's Rollickin' Roadsters (Cars Land).

Must-See California Adventure

1. **Radiator Springs Racers FastPass** ("a bug's land")
   The FastPass distribution is located near "It's Tough to be a Bug!" (not in Cars Land). You won't ride the Racers just yet.
2. **World of Color FastPass** (Grizzly Peak)
   Distribution is located next to the Grizzly River Run. The World of Color FastPass™ won't affect or be affected by other passes.
3. **Soarin'** (Grizzly Peak)
4. **Animation Academy** (Hollywood Land)
5. **Frozen – Live at the Hyperion** (Hollywood Land)
6. **Heimlich's Chew Chew Train** ("a bug's land)
7. *It's Tough to be a Bug!* ("a bug's land)
8. **Radiator Springs Racers** (Cars Land)
   use your FastPass
9. **The Bakery Tour** (Pacific Wharf)
10. **The Little Mermaid** – Ariel's Undersea Adventure (Paradise Pier)
11. **California Screamin'** (Paradise Pier)
12. **Toy Story Midway Mania®** (Paradise Pier)
13. **Mickey's Fun Wheel** (Paradise Pier)
14. **World of Color** (Paradise Pier)

*Guardians of the Galaxy – Mission: Breakout will open in Spring/Summer 2017. Make sure you reserve a FastPass first thing, possibly instead of Radiator Springs Racers.

Have more time? Check out the Silly Symphony Swings (Paradise Pier) or Goofy's Sky School (Paradise Pier).

With Kids Ages 6-10

1. **Radiator Springs Racers FastPass** ("a bug's land")
   The FastPass distribution is located near "It's Tough to be a Bug!" (not in Cars Land). You won't ride the Racers just yet.
2. **World of Color FastPass** (Grizzly Peak)
   Distribution is located next to the Grizzly River Run. The World of Color FastPass™ won't affect or be affected by other passes.
3. **Soarin'** (Grizzly Peak)
4. ***It's Tough to be a Bug!*** ("a bug's land")
5. **The Little Mermaid** - Ariel's Undersea Adventure (Paradise Pier)
6. **Mater's Junkyard Jamboree** (Cars Land)
7. **Radiator Springs Racers** (Cars Land)
8. **Toy Story Midway Mania®** (Paradise Pier)
9. **Mickey's Fun Wheel** (Paradise Pier)
10. **Silly Symphony Swings** (Paradise Pier)
11. **Goofy's Sky School** (Paradise Pier)
12. **Animation Academy** (Hollywood Land)
13. **Frozen - Live at the Hyperion** (Hollywood Land)
14. **Monsters Inc., Mike and Sulley to the Rescue!** (Hollywood Land)
15. **World of Color** (Paradise Pier)

Note: If your child enjoys faster rides, consider the following: Add California Screamin' between Radiator Springs Racers (7) and Toy Story Midway Mania (8).

With Kids Ages 2-5

1. **World of Color FastPass** (Grizzly Peak)
   Distribution is located next to the Grizzly River Run.
2. ***Redwood Creek Challenge Trail** (Grizzly Peak)
3. ***The Little Mermaid** - Ariel's Undersea Adventure (Paradise Pier)
4. ****It's Tough to be a Bug!*** ("a bug's land")
5. ***Heimlich's Chew Chew Train** ("a bug's land")
6. **Flik's Flyers** ("a bug's land")
7. **Francis' Ladybug Boogie** ("a bug's land")
8. ****Turtle Talk with Crush*** (Hollywood Land)
9. **Disney Junior - Live on Stage!** (Hollywood Land)
10. ***Monsters Inc., Mike and Sulley to the Rescue!** (Hollywood Land)
11. **Red Car Trolley** (Buena Vista Street)
12. **World of Color** (Paradise Pier)

*Attractions we recommend the most for preschoolers.

We understand that a list like this may not be so cut and dry when it comes to dealing with a fickle preschool-aged child. We recommend spreading out each attraction, and if you're met with resistance, venture into a gift shop, grab a snack, or enjoy the sights of Disney California Adventure - or head back to the hotel for a nap. Even if you only get the attractions with a * next to it, you've had a successful and memorable day!

Both Parks in One Day

Thrill Riders

1. Start at Disneyland
2. **Space Mountain FastPass** (Tomorrowland)
   The FastPass distribution is located to the right of the ride's queue. You won't ride Space Mountain just yet.
3. **Star Tours** (Tomorrowland)
4. **Buzz Lightyear Astro Blasters** (Tomorrowland)
5. **Matterhorn Bobsleds** (Fantasyland)
   Ask to the cast member if you can ride the left side rollercoaster (Tomorrowland side) for the faster speeds.
6. **Mad Tea Party** (Fantasyland)
7. **Sleeping Beauty Castle Walkthrough** (Fantasyland)
8. **Space Mountain** (Tomorrowland) *use FastPass*
9. **Indiana Jones Adventure FastPass** (Adventureland)
10. **Splash Mountain** (Critter Country)
11. **The Haunted Mansion** (New Orleans Square)
12. **Big Thunder Mountain Railroad** (Frontierland)
13. **Pirates of the Caribbean** (New Orleans Square)
14. **Indiana Jones Adventure** (Adventureland) *use FastPass*
15. Move to Disney California Adventure
16. **Soarin' FastPass** (Grizzly Peak)
17. **California Screamin'** (Paradise Pier)
18. **Toy Story Midway Mania®** (Paradise Pier)
19. **Goofy's Sky School** (Paradise Pier)
20. **Soarin'** (Grizzly Peak) *use FastPass*
21. **Radiator Springs Racers** (Cars Land) *Single Rider Line*
22. Back to Disneyland
23. **Disneyland Fireworks** (Main Street, U.S.A.)

Must-See Disneyland Resort Adventure

1. Start at Disneyland
2. **Space Mountain FastPass** (Tomorrowland)
   The FastPass distribution is to the right of the ride's queue.
3. **Star Tours** (Tomorrowland)
4. **Matterhorn Bobsleds** (Tomorrowland)
5. **Peter Pan's Flight** (Fantasyland)
6. **Mad Tea Party** (Fantasyland)
7. **"it's a small world"** (Fantasyland)
8. **Mickey or Minnie's House** (Mickey's Toontown)
9. **Space Mountain** (Tomorrowland) *use FastPass*
10. **Indiana Jones Adventure FastPass** (Adventureland)
11. **Jungle Cruise** (Adventureland)
12. **Pirates of the Caribbean** (New Orleans Square)
13. **Splash Mountain** (Critter Country)
14. **The Haunted Mansion** (New Orleans Square)
15. **Big Thunder Mountain Railroad** (Frontierland)
16. **Indiana Jones** (Adventureland) *use FastPass*
17. Move to California Adventure
18. **Soarin' FastPass** (Grizzly Peak)
15. **Animation Academy** (Hollywood Land)
16. *It's Tough to be a Bug!* ("a bug's land)
17. **Radiator Springs Racers** (Cars Land) *Single Rider line*
18. **The Little Mermaid** - Ariel's Undersea Adventure (Paradise Pier)
19. **California Screamin'** (Paradise Pier)
20. **Toy Story Midway Mania®** (Paradise Pier)
21. Back to Disneyland
22. **Disneyland Fireworks** (Main Street, U.S.A.)

With Kids Ages 6-10

1. Start at Disney California Adventure
2. **Radiator Springs Racers FastPass** ("a bug's land")
   The FastPass distribution is located near "It's Tough to be a Bug!" (not in Cars Land). You won't ride the Racers just yet.
3. **Soarin'** (Grizzly Peak)
4. *It's Tough to be a Bug!* ("a bug's land)
5. **The Little Mermaid** – Ariel's Undersea Adventure (Paradise Pier)
6. **Mater's Junkyard Jamboree** (Cars Land)
7. **Radiator Springs Racers** (Cars Land) *use FastPass*
8. **Toy Story Midway Mania®** (Paradise Pier)
9. **Mickey's Fun Wheel** (Paradise Pier)
10. **Silly Symphony Swings** (Paradise Pier)
11. **Goofy's Sky School** (Paradise Pier)
12. Move to Disneyland
13. **Peter Pan's Flight** (Fantasyland)
14. **Mr. Toad's Wild Ride** (Fantasyland)
15. **Gadget's Go-Coaster** (Mickey's Toontown)
16. **Roger Rabbit's Car Toon Spin** (Toontown)
17. **Mad Tea Party** (Fantasyland)
18. **Buzz Lightyear Astro Blasters** (Tomorrowland)
19. **Star Wars Launch Bay** (Tomorrowland)
    Meet the cuddly Chewbacca or the scary Kylo Ren
20. **Tarzan's Treehouse™** (Adventureland)
21. **Pirates of the Caribbean** (New Orleans Square)
22. **Paint the Night Parade** (Main Street, U.S.A.)
23. **Disneyland Fireworks** (Main Street, U.S.A.)

Notes: For faster rides, replace Mickey's Fun Wheel (9) with California Screamin' and Mr. Toad's Wild Ride (7) with The Matterhorn Bobsleds.

With Kids Ages 2-5

1. Start at Disneyland
2. *Peter Pan's Flight (Fantasyland)
3. *Dumbo the Flying Elephant (Fantasyland)
4. Bibbidi Bobbidi Boutique (Fantasyland)
   or ride the Casey Jr. Circus Train
5. Fantasy Faire (Fantasyland)
   Meet a princess and/or see a short theatre show
6. *Alice in Wonderland (Fantasyland)
7. *"it's a small world" (Fantasyland)
8. *Finding Nemo Submarine Voyage (Tomorrowland)
9. Tarzan's Treehouse™ (Adventureland)
10. *The Little Mermaid - Ariel's Undersea Adventure (Paradise Pier)
11. *It's Tough to be a Bug! ("a bug's land)
12. *Heimlich's Chew Chew Train ("a bug's land")
13. *Turtle Talk with Crush (Hollywood Land)
14. *Monsters Inc., Mike and Sulley to the Rescue! (Hollywood Land)
15. Back to Disneyland
16. *Paint the Night Parade (Main Street, U.S.A.)
17. Disneyland Fireworks (Main Street, U.S.A.)

*Attractions we recommend the most for preschoolers.
We understand that a list (and running between both parks) may not be so cut and dry when it comes to dealing with a fickle young child. We recommend spreading out each attraction, venture into a gift shop, grab a snack, or enjoy the sights of the parks- or head back to the hotel for a nap. Even if you only get the attractions with a * next to it, you've had a successful and memorable day!

Custom Ride List:

Names: _____   _____
       _____   _____
       _____   _____

1. _____
2. _____
3. _____
4. _____
5. _____
6. _____
7. _____
8. _____
9. _____
10. _____
11. _____
12. _____
13. _____
14. _____
15. _____
16. _____
17. _____
18. _____
19. _____
20. _____
21. _____
22. _____
23. _____
24. _____
25. _____

Custom Ride List:

Names: _____   _____
       _____   _____
       _____   _____

1. _____
2. _____
3. _____
4. _____
5. _____
6. _____
7. _____
8. _____
9. _____
10. _____
11. _____
12. _____
13. _____
14. _____
15. _____
16. _____
17. _____
18. _____
19. _____
20. _____
21. _____
22. _____
23. _____
24. _____
25. _____

Disneyland Resort Vacation Checklist

- ❑ Park Tickets
- ❑ Ride List
- ❑ ID
- ❑ Credit Card / Cash
- ❑ Hotel Address
- ❑ Phone (and charging cable)
- ❑ Sunscreen
- ❑ Toiletries: toothbrush, toothpaste, etc.
- ❑ Swimsuit
- ❑ Jacket
- ❑ Comfortable Shoes
- ❑ Plastic bag for cellphone (water rides)
- ❑ Snacks
- ❑ Water bottles (if you aren't flying)
- ❑ Backpack or bag
- ❑ Restaurant Reservations
- ❑ Disneyland Guide Book by Magic Guides
- ❑ _____
- ❑ _____
- ❑ _____
- ❑ _____
- ❑ _____
- ❑ _____
- ❑ _____
- ❑ _____
- ❑ _____
- ❑ _____

Index

A

adult guide, 148–158
Adventureland, 76-79, 140
air conditioning, 14, 83, 99, 150
alcoholic beverages, 51, 103, 153
Alice in Wonderland, 89-90, 107
AMC 12 (movies), 128, 156
Anabella hotel, The, 68
Anaheim, 42, 46
Anaheim Train Station, 46
Animation Academy, 105, 168
Annual Pass, 41
Ariel's Grotto, 117-119, 153
attractions,
    for babies and toddlers, 135-137
    for kids, 138-147
    for thrill riders, 187, 191, 195
Award Wieners, 106
author, information, 8
Autopia, 98, 137, 142

B

Baby Care Center, The Disneyland, 134-135
babysitters, 149
Bakery Tour, 111
Bats Day, 26-27
Bayside Brews, 120, 153
Beauty and the Beast (stage show), 92
Bengal Barbecue, 33,
best days to visit, 35, 76, 79, 140
Bibbidi Bobbidi Boutique, 93, 160
Big Thunder Mountain Railroad, 80, 137, 141, 163

Blue Bayou restaurant, 33, 84-85, 155
Boardwalk Pizza and Pasta, 145
boats rides,
    Finding Nemo Submarine Voyage, 97, 142, 155
    Grizzly River Run, 49, 58, 120-122, 147, 157, 165
    "it's a small world", 14, 24, 33, 91, 135, 161
    Jungle Cruise, 24, 33, 77, 136
    Pirates of the Caribbean, 83, 136, 141
    Columbia, Sailing Ship, 81
    Splash Mountain, 49-50, 86-87, 137, 139, 164-165
    Storybook Land Canal Boats, 91, 139, 175
Boudin Bakery, 111-112, 168
both parks in one day, 82-86
breast feeding, 135
Buena Vista Street, 52, 102-104
Buffets, 61-62, 64, 66, 75
"bug's land", "a", 101, 107-108, 136, 143
bumper cars (see Tuck and Roll's Drive 'Em Buggies)
Build-A-Bear Workshop, 127
Buzz Lightyear Astro Blasters, 98, 142, 155, 164, 172

C

cabs (see taxi)
Café Orleans, 33, 85, 141
Cafeteria style, 13, 100, 142

California Adventure (see Disney California Adventure)
California Screamin', 13, 113, 137, 166
camera, 87, 92, 168
Candy Cane Inn, 68
Car Toon Spin (see Rodger Rabbit's Car Toon Spin)
car, driving by, 43-44
Carnation Café, The, 75, 138
Cars Land, 101, 108-110, 145-146
Carthay Circle Lounge, 103, 151, 153
Carthay Circle Restaurant, 102-103, 117, 153
Casey Jr. Circus Train, 91, 139
cash, 50
Catal Restaurant, 124, 153
cats inside of Disneyland, 178, 183
Character Dining, 38-39, 118, 130
character locations, 130-132
checklist, 201
Child Swap (see Rider Switch)
Children (see kids)
Chip N' Dale Treehouse, 96, 140
chocolate (see Ghirardelli Soda Fountain & Chocolate Shop)
Christmas, 23, 32-34, 77, 83, 132
CityPASS, 40-41
Clarabelle's, 96, 104, 143
Club 33, 182
Cocina Cucamonga Mexican Grill, 111, 145
Columbia Ship, 81
corn dog, 82, 119-120
Corn Dog Castle, 119-120, 171
cost,
    hotel, 84
    food (see dining)
    park tickets, 16
    parking, 67
Courtyard Marriott Anaheim Theme Park, 67-68
Cozy Cone Motel, 110, 146
credit cards, 50
Critter Country, 86-88, 139-140

D

Daisy's Diner, 96
Dapper Dans, 162
Dapper Day, 27, 32
Del Sol Inn, 69
dining
    adults, 216-220
    Disneyland, 75-100
    Disney California Adventure, 102-122
    Downtown Disney, 124-127
    general information, 15
    hotel, 61-67
    kids, 138-147
    reservations, 15
discounts, booking with, 16
Disney, Walt, 10, 56, 70-71, 81, 102, 133, 173, 184
Disney Animation, 105, 146
Disney California Adventure,
    Buena Vista Street, 102-104
    "bug's land", "a", 107-108
    Cars Land, 108-110
    Grizzly Peak, 120-122
    history, 101
    Hollywood Land, 104-106
    hotel (see Disney's Grand Californian)
    Pacific Wharf, 110-112
    Paradise Pier, 113-120
    tickets, 16
    shows, 105, 108, 111, 116-118
Disneyland fireworks, 71-73
Disneyland Hotel, 54, 56-57
Disneyland Park,
    Adventureland, 76-79
    Critter Country, 86-88
    Fantasyland, 88-94
    fireworks, 71-73
    Frontierland, 79-82
    Main Street, U.S.A., 71-76
    Mickey's Toontown, 94-96
    New Orleans Square, 82-86
    shows, 74, 78, 92-93, 95, 99
    tickets, 16
    Tomorrowland, 96-100

Disneyland Railroad, 18, 74, 136
Disneyland Resort
      booking, 15-16, 34-41
      hotels, 53-69
      tickets, 16
disneyland.com, 55-56
dogs, 51
Dole whip, 63, 78-79
Donald Duck, 130
Downtown Disney, 123-128
D-Street, 127
Dumbo the Flying Elephant, 89, 135

E

Earl of Sandwich, 124
early entry (see Extra Magic Hours)
eating (see Restaurants)
edible plants, Tomorrowland, 183
Elias and Company Department Store, 24, 33, 177
Enchanted Tiki Room, 78
entertainment (see shows)
esplanade, 157
ESPN Zone, 123-124, 152-153
exchange, currency, 50
Expedia.com, 54
Extra Magic Hours, 37, 55, 71

F

family rides, 170
Fantasmic!, 18, 83-84
Fantasy Faire, 92-93, 138
Fantasyland, 88-94
Fantasyland Theatre, 93
FastPass, 14-15, 163-166
Fiddler, Fifer, and Practical Café, 103
Finding Nemo Submarine Voyage, 97, 142
fireworks, 71-73
first aid, 135
Flik's Fun Fair, 107, 143
Flo's V8 Café, 109-110, 146
food (see restaurants)

French Market, 33, 85-86
Frontierland, 79-82
Frozen, 93, 105
Frozen – Live at the Hyperion, 105

G

Gadget's Go Coaster, 95
Galactic Grill, 100, 142-143
games, 117-118, 123-124
Gay Days, 29, 31
Ghirardelli Soda Fountain & Chocolate Shop, 111-112
Gibson Girl Ice Cream Parlor, 31, 33, 76, 138
Golden Horseshoe, The, 34, 79, 81, 141
Golden Zephyr, 116, 144
Goofy's Kitchen, 61
Goofy's Playhouse, 96, 140
Goofy's Sky School, 115-116, 137, 144, 156, 164, 166
Great Moments with Mr. Lincoln, 74
Grizzly Peak, 120, 147, 157, 165
Grizzly River Run, 58, 122, 137, 147
Guardians of the Galaxy – Mission: Breakout, 17, 104, 164

H

Halloween, 29-31
hamburgers, 143, 147,
Harbour Galley, 88
Haunted Mansion, 24, 30, 33, 83
Haunted Mansion Holiday, 24, 30, 33, 83
Heimlich's Chew Chew Train, 107, 136,143
Hidden Mickeys, 143-179
holiday treats, 33-34
holidays, 22
Hollywood Land, 104-106
hopper tickets, park, 14, 16, 36-37
hot dogs, 96, 106, 119-120, 140, 147
hotels, 53-69

Hungry Bear Restaurant, 87-88, 140
Hyatt Regency Orange County hotel, 68
Hyperion Theater, 105
Hyperspace Mountain, 18-19, 97, 142, 164

I

ice cream, 31, 33, 76, 96, 104, 120, 127, 138
Indiana Jones Adventure, 76-77, 137, 140, 163, 165
"it's a small world", 14, 24, 33, 91-92, 135
It's Tough to be a Bug!, 108, 143

J

Jamba Juice, 123, 127
Jedi Training Academy, 99, 142
Jumpin' Jellyfish, 116, 137, 144, 156
Jingle Cruise (Jungle Cruise Holiday), 24, 33, 77
John Wayne Airport, 44-45, 47
Jungle Cruise, 24, 33, 76-77, 136, 161, 174, 181

K

kennels, pet, 51
King Arthur Carrousel, 91, 136, 175
King Triton's Carousel, 115, 136, 144, 156

L

La Brea Bakery Café, 125, 153
LAX (see Los Angeles International)
LEGO Store, The, 128
LEGOLAND, 41

Little Mermaid – Ariel's Undersea Adventure, 115, 144, 156
lockers, 52, 71
Los Angeles International, 35, 42-47
Lucky Fortune Cookery, 112, 145
Luigi's Rollickin' Roadsters, 137, 145
Lyft, 45-47

M

Mad Tea Party, 89-90, 139
Main Street Cinema, 74, 160
Main Street Electrical Parade, 18, 74
Main Street USA, 71-76
Many Adventures of Winnie the Pooh, The, 87, 90, 135, 139, 155, 164
maps, 167, 181
Marceline's Confectionery, 128
Mark Twain Riverboat, 80, 175
Market House, 31, 75, 176
Marvel, 17, 104, 129
Marvel characters, 132
Mary Poppins, 76
Mater's Junkyard Jamboree, 109. 137, 145
Matterhorn Bobsleds, 88-89, 137, 139, 154, 163, 165, 182
Mickey and the Magical Map, 93, 160
Mickey Mouse (character), 75, 82, 94, 131
Mickey's Fun Wheel, 101, 114-115, 117-118
Mickey's House, 177
Mickey's Toontown, 94-96, 136
military discounts, 39
Mickeys, Hidden, 173-179
Minnie's House, 9, 177
Mint Julep Bar, 86
money exchange, 50
monorail, 56-57, 60
Monsters, Inc. Mike and Sulley to the Rescue, 104, 146, 156
Mortimer's Fish Market, 104
motels (see hotels)
Mr. Toad's Wild Ride, 90, 139

N

Napa Rose Lounge, 65
Napa Rose restaurant, 64
Naples Ristorante e Pizzeria, 125, 153
Napolini, 125-126
Nemo (see Finding Nemo Submarine Voyage)
New Orleans Square, 82-86
Nightmare Before Christmas, The, 24, 30, 33, 83, 132

O

one day, both parks, 82-86
Orange County, 45, 68

P

Pacific Wharf, 110-112
Pacific Wharf Café, 122, 171
Paint the Night parade, 73, 78, 160
parades, 18, 30, 33, 52, 71, 73-74
Paradise Garden Grill, 119
Paradise Pier, 113-120
Park Hopper tickets, 14, 16, 36-37, 38
Parking, 447
PCH Grill, 92, 98
Peter Pan's Flight, 89, 140
pets (see kennels)
phone number list, 15-16
PierGames, 117-118
Pinocchio's Daring Journey, 91, 140
Pinocchio's Workshop, 150
Pirates of the Caribbean, 83-84, 137, 142
Pirate's Lair on Tom Sawyer Island, 81, 142, 156
Pixar Play Parade, 144
pizza, 96, 100, 106, 125-126, 141, 143, 146
planning,
	checklist, 202
	hotels, 33-69
Plaza Inn, 34, 75, 139

Pluto's Dog House, 96
Priceline.com, 40, 43
prices (see cost)
princesses, Disney, 33, 92-93, 107, 129-132, 143, 160, 183
Princess Dot Puddle Park, 107, 143

Q

Quiksilver, 128

R

Radiator Springs Racers, 101, 108-109, 137, 146, 165-166
rafts (see Tom Sawyer's Island)
railroads,
	Anaheim Station, 46
	Big Thunder Mountain Railroad, 80, 137, 141, 163
	Casey Jr. Circus Train, 91, 139
	Disneyland Railroad, 18, 74, 136
	Heimlich's Chew Chew Train, 107, 136, 143
rain, 50
Rainforest Café, 125, 128
Ralph Brennan's Jazz Kitchen, 126, 153
Rancho del Zocalo Restaurante, 30, 82, 175
Red Car Trolley, 102, 143, 156
Redd Rockett's Pizza Port, 142
Redwood Creek Challenge Trail, 122, 156
Refreshment Corner, 33, 76
reservations,
	hotel, 15
	restaurant, 15-16
restrooms, 49, 107, 135, 158
RIDEMAKERZ, 128
Rider Switch, 137
rides (see attractions)
River Belle Terrace, 81-82
Rivers of America, 79, 81-82, 85, 88

Roger Rabbit's Car Toon Spin, 95, 140, 164
roller coasters,
> Big Thunder Mountain Railroad, 80, 137, 141, 163
> California Screamin', 13, 113, 137, 166
> Gadget's Go Coaster, 95
> Goofy's Sky School, 115-116, 137, 144, 156, 164, 166
> Matterhorn Bobsleds, 88-89, 137, 139, 154, 163, 165, 182
> Space Mountain, 18-19, 30, 72, 97, 137, 142, 164
> Space Mountain: Ghost Galaxy, 30

Royal Hall at Fantasy Faire, 92-93, 138
Royal Street Veranda, 34, 86
Royal Theatre at Fantasy Faire, 92-93, 138

S

Santa Claus, 24, 32, 33
Sanuk, 128
Season of the Force, 19, 96
selfie sticks, 51
Sephora, 128, 156, 158
Shootin' Exposition, Frontierland, 80
shuttles, 44-45, 68
Silly Symphony Swings, 115, 137, 144, 156
Single Rider Line, 15, 77, 109, 165-166
Sleeping Beauty Castle, 72-73, 92
slow-moving rides, 160-161, 170
Smokejumpers Grill, 122, 147
smoking sections, 157-158
Snow White's Scary Adventures, 90, 139
Soarin', 120-121, 137, 147, 165-166, 178
Something Silver, 128
Sorcerer's Workshop, 105, 146
Space Mountain, 18-19, 30, 72, 97, 137, 142, 164

Space Mountain: Ghost Galaxy, 30
Splash Mountain, 49-50, 86-87, 137, 139, 164-165
Stage Door Café, 82
Star Tours – The Adventures Continue, 97, 142, 164, 170, 177
Star Wars, 17-19, 96-97, 99-100
Star Wars Land, 17-18
Star Wars Launch Bay, 99
Starbucks, 35, 67, 75, 103
Steakhouse, 62-63, 151
storage (see lockers)
Storybook Land Canal Boats, 91, 139, 175
Storyteller's Café, 61, 130
Strollers, 49, 134
Sunglass Icon, 128

T

Tangaroa Terrace, 62
Tangled (lvie show), 92-93
Tarzan's Treehouse, 77-78, 155
taxis, 47
terms (see phrases)
tickets, 16, 40-41
Tiki Juice Bar, 79
thrill rides, 187, 191, 195
Tom Sawyer Island, 81, 155
Tomorrowland, 96-100
Tomorrowland Terrace (see Galactic Grill)
Tomorrowland Theater, 99
Tortilla Jo's, 126, 153
tours, 184
Toy Story Midway Mania!, 113-114, 144
Trader Sam's Enchanted Tiki Bar, 56, 62, 150, 154
trains (see railroads)
travel packages, 16, 3-41
trolley, 102, 143, 156
Troubadour Tavern, 94
Tuck and Roll's Drive 'Em Buggies, 107, 137, 143
Turtle Talk with Crush, 105, 146
Twilight Zone Tower of Terror, 17

U

umbrellas, 50, 137
Uva Bar, 127, 153

V

Village Haus, 34, 94, 139

W

walking distance, hotels within, 54, 55, 60, 67-69

Walt Disney, 10, 56, 70-71, 81, 102, 133, 173, 184
Walt Disney Company, 8
Walt Disney World, 8, 10-11
water bottles, 49
weather, 20-25
websites, 16, 38, 40, 54-55
Wine Country Trattoria, 112, 117, 152-153
WonderGround Gallery, 128
World of Color, 24, 33, 114-119, 144, 152, 160, 162, 165
World of Disney (store), 123, 127

Z

Zocalo Restaurante, Rancho Del, 30, 82, 175

Conclusion

Thank you for the purchase of this guide. We sincerely hope that this book is a valuable resource for you. As noted at the beginning, we are Disneyland fans and we've created this book from our firsthand knowledge and research over many years and countless visits.

Walt Disney once said: "Disneyland will never be completed. It will continue to grow as long as there is imagination left in the world."

We feel the same way about our guide books! Each edition is specific for the year and will contain information reviewing the attractions of the time. In the future, we plan to add more and give more to you!

Also Available

MAGIC GUIDEBOOKS 2017 GUIDE
Walt Disney World®

Secrets, Money Saving Tips, Hidden Mickeys, and Everything Else You Need to Know!
We help you plan in this complete guide to the Walt Disney World Resort Reviews and tips for the Attractions, Restaurants, Hotels, and Beyond

www.magicguidebooks.com

Want Free Stuff?

From more free tips, booking discounts, and more for your Disney vacation?

Sign up for our FREE e-mail list

Visit:
www.magicguidebooks.com/disneyland

OR

Scan this code with your mobile device:

Note: *we believe in privacy and will never solicit your information.*

Wishing you a magical vacation!
Magic Guidebooks

Made in the USA
Lexington, KY
27 March 2017